SMALL ANTIQUE FURNITURE

Portrait of Queen Anne in wax and paper filigree. The intricate elaborations of dress and background are composed of tiny rolls and scrolls of gilt and coloured paper. About 1710.

BERNARD AND THERLE HUGHES

SMALL
ANTIQUE FURNITURE

FREDERICK A. PRAEGER, *Publishers*
New York · Washington

BOOKS THAT MATTER
Published in the United States of America in 1968
by Frederick A. Praeger, Inc., Publishers
111 Fourth Avenue, New York, N.Y. 10003
First published in the United States in 1959
by the Macmillan Co., New York, N.Y.

© 1958 in London, England, by G. Bernard Hughes and Therle Hughes

Library of Congress Catalog Card Number: 68-21581

PRINTED IN GREAT BRITAIN

CONTENTS

PLATES

7

8

LIST OF ILLUSTRATIONS

DRAWINGS

Chapter One

THE ORIGIN OF HOUSE-FURNISHERS

YESTERDAY as today the house-furnisher made an impressive contribution to the English art of gracious living. Joiner, cabinet-maker, upholsterer, chair-maker, pewterer and the other essential old-time craftsmen are familiar figures to those who delight in turning back the pages of social history. But it quickly becomes apparent that even by Elizabethan days the liaison between these specialists and the buying public, the universal expert, the exponent of elegance and arbiter of good taste, was the comparatively obscure house-furnisher. Cotgrave even used the modern name as early as 1611. House furnishing on a grand scale was almost unknown until Elizabethan days. But with newly acquired wealth came an immense delight in its magnificent display. The house-furnisher's establishment and rise to considerable eminence was tacit recognition that not only splendour and elegance but grace and comfort had become matters of importance in an ever-widening range of homes.

William Harrison in 1587 recorded his personal impressions of this great social change, occurring not only in the houses of "the nobility and gentry, but also of the lowest sort in most places of our south country. . . . In the houses of knights, gentlemen, merchant men and other wealthy citizens one now beholds tapestry, Turkey work, pewter, brass, fine linen, costly cupboards of silver plate. Farmers also have learned to garnish their cupboards with plate, their joined beds with tapestry hangings, and their tables with fine carpets and napery."

The obvious result of such awakened interest was the establishment of the house-furnisher, displaying under a single roof an extensive range of goods acquired from joiner, pewterer, embroiderer and so on. In particular he would be the man to fill the countless smaller needs that would transform house into home, the important minor furniture that forms the subject of this book. He it was who created demand as well as meeting it and his taste and good sense considerably guided design and craftsmanship, so that no consideration of such peculiarly collectable antiques may be considered complete without some understanding of his trade.

His warehouse was a timber building of plain gable style, "a greate cellar beneath, a high loft above". The loft comprised of two floors above ground level with attic rooms in the gables. Half of the street frontage was occupied by two or three small display windows. The other half was fitted with wide folding doors with a portable counter in front of them, standing on large paving stones some feet wide, at a period when the roadway itself would probably be paved with large smooth-surfaced cobbles known as thunderbolt stones. Shop-keepers were required to keep the roadway before their premises clean and it was unlawful to sweep their rubbish in front of their neighbours' premises.

The counter was afforded some protection from the weather by a wooden awning extending from the façade: later this was of lath and plaster. Here the shopman stood calling his wares and in daylight showing them to his customers. But in the long working day of that period much business had to be transacted after dark, the counter carried indoors and the shop but poorly lit by several foul-smelling multi-flame whale-oil cruses.

House-furnishers were open at 7 a.m., an apprentice sweeping the roadway and cleaning the timber of the shop-front before wares were set out for display on the pavement. At noon there was an hour for a midday meal, the master usually taking charge of the shop, which remained open until 8 o'clock in the evening and until midnight on Saturday, with no half-holiday—a 76-hour week for the shopmen. Unmarried employees and apprentices lived in the gable rooms, with no means of escape in case of fire.

London-made furniture of good quality was "joined" and so highly valued that inventories of middle-class homes

"The Hilliard Family of Cowley Manor at Tea", by Karl Anton Hickel. The satinwood tea-tray is set with blue and white Caughley porcelain, silver cream jug and veneered tea-chest.

Plate 1
"William Ferguson celebrating his succession to Raith", by Johann Zoffany, 1781. The champagne bottles stand in a brass-hooped mahogany wine cistern with moulded legs and corner brackets. The claw table has the low-curving legs of its period.

Plate 2
(*Top*) London House: Seddon's showrooms facing Aldersgate in the 1780s. A three-winged factory was at the rear. (*Below*) Fashionable furniture of 1809 displayed in the showrooms of Morgan and Sanders in Catherine Street, Strand: Pitt's cabinet globe writing-table is seen in the centre. From *Ackermann's Repository of the Arts.*

throughout the country distinguished between the joiner-made furniture and the much more frequent "boarded" furniture made by local carpenters.

In even less affluent homes people had long been satisfied to sleep on "straw pallets or rough mats, covered only with a sheet and a coverlet of hop harlot, with a good round log under their heads for pillows". Now they were developing a taste for the inexpensive "boarded furniture". John Stow in his *Survey of London*, 1598, noted that such furniture was sold by dealers in second-hand goods known as upholders, who were also undertakers. Upholders were frequently furniture-makers, but those who specialised in the sale of furnishing textiles and stuffed furniture were upholsterers. Samuel Pepys in 1668 fluently described a visit he and his wife made to an upholsterer in Long Lane when about to acquire new hangings for their four-poster bed.

House-furnishers became highly important and prosperous tradesmen during the time of Charles II when the joiner gave way to the more highly skilled cabinet-maker and printed linens came into vogue. Luxury and splendour became more widespread and a great change took place in interior decoration. All who could afford to do so refurnished throughout in the new styles. The premises of leading tradesmen necessarily became more extensive and late in the century the term "furniture gallery" appeared. The frontages of such premises were enriched with masses of elaborately carved oak, foliated ornament being usual. The living premises on the first floor were approached by a private entrance from the street, the shop door being placed between a pair of capacious three-sided display windows, three times as high as formerly.

House-furnishers usually expended a considerable amount of money on a shop sign which swung from a massive decorative bracket of wrought iron over the roadway. This might be a model of some article of furniture or a board painted on both sides with an emblem symbolic of the trade such as the three tents of the Upholders' Company used by Henry Newton. These designs in bright colours and gold, enclosed in heavy carved and gilded frames, were also reproduced on trade cards and bill heads.

Serious fires were a considerable hazard on premises engaged in branches of the furnishing trade. Their frequency made fire-insurance premiums extremely high and premiums on timber buildings were double those on brick and stone premises. From about 1710 it became a law that all traders storing inflammable materials should be housed in buildings with stone or brick walls.

The more progressive house-furnishers, of course, were already occupying premises as fireproof as knowledge at that period made possible. Thus, for several years William Overly occupied the ground floor of the Leadenhall Street entrance of the old East India House. But he moved to less flimsy premises nearby, issuing a trade card that showed East India House with his former shop, and announcing that he made joined furniture including "presses in Deal and Wainscot, and Bedstids, Tables, Desks, Book Cases, Burows and Writing Desks".

Stone-built house-furnishing premises of the early Georgian period usually consisted of a tall vaulted ware-house, with rooms opening to right and left and with cellars below. The front opened to the street with folding doors extending to the full height of the shop and secured within by heavy iron bars and massive padlocks. There was also an expansive small-paned display window known as "the view". These show-rooms were extensive and divided into departments as in present-day stores with a specialist salesman in attendance at each.

The Georgian furniture salesman had indeed to be a man of parts. He was required to dress fashionably and neatly, to possess a wide knowledge of cabinet woods and textiles, and to be capable of discussing their arrangement in the home. Hours still remained at 76 and wages were twelve to fifteen shillings a week; women assistants, chiefly employed in sewing textiles, were paid a shilling a day, on a day-to-day basis. Workshops usually formed a separate block of buildings at the rear.

The *London Tradesman*, 1747, fully describes the activities of the early Georgian upholder, referring to him as the chief agent in house-furnishing. "Upon him I rely for the Choice of Goods for he has not only Judgment in the Material, but

Taste in the Fashions and Skill in the Workmanship. This tradesman's genius must be universal in every branch of furniture."

Considerable capital was required to set up in business and a first-class cabinet-maker was often financed. "A youth", advises the *London Tradesman*, "who designs to make a figure in this trade must learn to draw, for upon this depends the inventions of new fashions and upon that the success of his business. He who first hits upon any new whim is sure to make by the invention before it becomes common in trade; but he that must always wait for a new fashion till it comes from Paris is never likely to grow rich."

England's rapidly increasing wealth in the eighteenth century brought with it a country-wide demand for fine houses and luxurious furnishings. The activities of the fashionable mid-Georgian retail furnisher were immeasurably expanded: in addition to a flair for buying and selling he was required to possess a working knowledge of interior decoration. Schools of industrial art were established in London and Birmingham, experienced masters being obtained from France, Italy and Germany. More than fifty of these continental instructors were fully occupied in Birmingham by 1762. Retail furnishers were first among those eager for tuition in design and colour arrangement.

Minor artists might find employment as designers among a few of the larger firms, such as Edward Edwards, A.R.A., who "drew patterns for furniture" for William Hallett (1707–1781). Smaller firms might allocate such designing to free-lance artists experienced in this work: in other cases it was carried out by the master or the head carver who, as a branch of his craft, could produce working drawings. The result was that visitors to England between 1760 and the 1780s expressed admiration for the lovely homes of Londoners. A German visitor to the home of Warren Hastings wrote how impressed she was by the way "the reflection of the pink-and-white shimmering curtains with sea-green edgings and fringes, and the rich verdure of the trees outside gave the reception room an extremely pleasant light".

The furniture retailers of the 1780s revolutionised shop

window display by remodelling their frontages. Small panes set in a network of slender glazing bars were replaced by frames of white-painted woodwork fitted with newly invented cast plate glass, each pane measuring 8 feet by 5 feet, and, for the first time, crystal clear. Illumination at night was provided by Argand lamps, then outmoding the open-flame oil lamps of past centuries.

Within a year or so the evening brilliance of Oxford Street was such that it became a favourite resort for window gazing which became a fashionable after-dinner amusement, dinner then ending by about 6 o'clock. Furniture retailers displayed furniture constructed of colourful woods from the Indies, intricate inlay work, gorgeous oriental lacquers and radiant textiles. Silversmiths and jewellers offered sumptuous work in gold, silver and precious stones, and china dealers their enamelled porcelains and scintillating cut-glass. All these, and the silk, lace and fan shops too, became a source of unceasing wonderment to rich and poor alike.

When in the spring of 1786 Sophie von la Roche visited London she described the scene as she and her friends "strolled up and down lovely Oxford Street, for some goods look more attractive by artificial light. Just imagine a street taking half an hour to cover from end to end, with double rows of brightly shining lamps, in the inside of which stand an equally long row of beautiful coaches, and on either side of these there is room for two coaches to pass one another: and the pavement, inlaid with flagstones, can stand six people deep and allow one to gaze at the splendidly lit shop fronts in comfort." She was already acquainted with other continental capitals, yet reported to her home in Germany that the shops of Oxford Street were more handsomely impressive than elsewhere in Europe. No doubt she had paused admiringly before the windows at Gillows of No. 176; at James & Thomas Eyer's soft-furnishing display at No. 356 near the Pantheon; at carved furniture by George Leader exhibited in the window of No. 108; at the "four post and other bedsteads with damask, mohair, moreen, cotton and check furniture" erected by John and Robert Pringe in their window at the corner of Wardour Street.

Her astonishment at the brilliance of the evening illumina-

18

tion was emphasised: "there were reflecting lamps which intensified the glare to such an extent that my eye could scarce stand it a moment . . . it is almost impossible to express how well everything is organised in London shops. Every article is made more attractive to the eye than in Paris. We especially noticed a cunning device for showing textiles, which hang down in folds behind the fine high windows so that their effect can be studied."

The master cabinet-makers became increasingly aware that greater profits were to be made by retailing direct than through upholders. Thus encouraged they tended more and more to occupy premises with shop frontages and rear workshops. They became upholsterers too. Those establishments that succeeded quickly outgrew accommodation and by the 1780s it became customary for workshops to be separated widely from their retail stores. Typical were the businesses of Charles Pryor who from about 1782 until 1800 supplied his retail stores at No. 472 Strand with furniture made at his factory in Chelsea; and Oakley, Shackleton & Evans, "the most tasteful of London cabinet-makers", with a "magazine" at No. 8 Old Bond Street and a factory at No. 22 St. Paul's Church Yard.

An interesting sidelight on the retail furnishing trade of nearly two centuries ago is that modern phraseology was already in use. A trade card in the collection of Sir Ambrose Heal, issued in about 1790 by Robert Milligan, Mint Street, Southwark, announced that he "Furnishes Houses on easy terms". Press advertisements to this effect have been noted dating to the early 1770s. Another little-known branch of the trade was furniture hiring. Chippendale, for instance, hired card tables and rout chairs, and Stubbs in City Road stocked four thousand tables and chairs for this purpose. A temporary resident in London was able to rent a house for a few months and hire complete furnishings from certain upholders dealing in second-hand furniture.

Little advertising was done, an occasional inch in a newspaper being considered ample. Seldom did cabinet-makers sign their work even if sold directly to the user: four or five names have been noted engraved on brass labels dating to the 1790s. Trade bills printed on flimsy paper and pasted to the back of a piece or the underside of a table were probably more frequent than known examples might suggest, having been rubbed away by vigorous cleaning.

Cabinet-makers working exclusively in mahogany, walnut and exotic woods for their own retail shops were soon extending the scope of their output by selling less expensive furniture in wainscot (Baltic oak) and beech. This was sold by the more obscure retail furnishers and an ever-increasing trade was soon developed. By 1790 specialists in this popular furniture began to appear, some devoting their entire energies to carved chairs, others to turned chairs, to dining tables, small tables, and so on. These factories working entirely by manual processes produced innumerable identical pieces at highly competitive prices.

Steam power brought with it mass production on what was then considered to be an amazing scale. The first steam-driven lathe was installed in a cabinet-making factory at Southwark in 1806. By then hard cutting steel had been perfected so that tools no longer required continual regrinding, case-hardening and tempering. Formerly cutting steel could be hardened to a depth of little more than $\frac{1}{8}$ inch.

By the 1820s this development was carrying inexpensive furniture into the homes of every reasonably housed work-man enabling him to furnish at least a parlour and best bedroom in a comfortable style. Simultaneously textiles were produced in greater variety, at greater speed in vast quantities at a fraction of eighteenth-century prices.

All this brought into being a country-wide network of inexpensive retail furnishers catering for small homes and servants' rooms. Others set up as specialists in the retailing of "printed furniture fabrics", such as Mitchell's Print Ware-house in Leadenhall Street. The low prices resulting from mechanisation, the introduction of French polish in about 1820, and the demand for furniture chintz gave to the late Georgian furniture retailer a turnover hitherto believed unattainable.

Furniture parts could be obtained by the retail furnisher who might assemble and French polish them in his own workshops. Many an assistant was now able to establish himself in business with a fraction of the capital formerly

Plate 3

Knife, fork and spoon box in veneered mahogany with satinwood ornament; late eighteenth century. Teapoy in mahogany with octagonal top, turned pillar, low tripod. Walnut tripod polescreen with turned shaft and pad feet; 1750s. Tea-chest in light tortoiseshell containing three mahogany canisters; late eighteenth century. Work table of mahogany inlaid with satinwood lines, with a square pull-out pouch under the drawer and a shelf below; late eighteenth century.

Plate 4

(*Top and upper left and right*) A writing-cum-Pembroke table made after 1798 by George Seddon, Sons and Shackleton, London House, Aldersgate, and bearing the Seddon label as shown. When the central cord is pulled the pigeon holes and drawers rise at the back as shown; when the two other cords are pulled a reading-desk with drawers and candlestick rest rises. This desk was patented by Day Gunby. (*Lower left*) Mahogany "chest of drawers mirror" exported by the Seddon firm in 1793 to Niels Aalls, Ulefoss Manor House, near Porsgrunn, Norway. (*Lower right*) Walnut toilet mirror with turned supports and swivel fitment, rising from a miniature bureau; early eighteenth century.

necessary to provide an adequate stock of hand-made goods. Some of these establishments were extensive: fashionable plate-glass shop fronts were backed with roof-lighted warehouses, often galleried. The only change in the assistants' former condition was a slight reduction in hours, opening at 8 a.m. and closing at 8 p.m., and at 11 p.m. on Saturday, a total of 69 hours. The average wage was a guinea a week.

Much trade was secured by personal recommendation such as was given by the wife of Sir Thomas Hardy, the officer who was at Nelson's side when he died. When William Creevey wished to furnish his rooms she wrote to him on 14th September 1834: "Sir Thomas says you wished to know from me the address of an upholsterer that would be less expensive, and equally good as the fashionable ones. . . . There is a good repository for furniture nearly opposite Conduit Street in Regent Street. I think the name is Willan and Hart, but it is an open warehouse with a great deal of furniture in the door and window. I bought some and found them reasonable and *good*. For objects of *Taste* and good bedding &c. I employ *Tratt and Atfield* in Lower Brook Street, and found them very civil and more reasonable than I expected, but not what could be called *bargains.*"

Chapter Two

THE FURNITURE-MAKER'S WORKSHOP

THE house-furnisher of yesterday who sold today's furniture antiques was the more likely to suceed if he were also a manufacturer. To complete the picture of how minor furniture antiques came into existence this chapter describes something of the workshops, equipment, methods and stock of three considerable firms, ranging in date from the mid-eighteenth century to the end of the Regency years, all notably successful because they made it their purpose to understand the peculiar needs of their many minor clients as well as furnishing the stately mansions of the wealthy few. Chippendale, the Seddon family and Morgan & Sanders have been chosen because their names are generally familiar and some of their work identified, yet the approach hitherto has been mainly academic. No one previously, it appears, has endeavoured to go through the goods entrance or behind the counters and view their premises as factories or their contact with the public in terms of commercial enterprise.

Thomas Chippendale (1718–1779), son of an obscure master-joiner in Otley, Yorkshire, acquired his remarkable posthumous reputation among Georgian furniture designers and cabinet-makers chiefly because of *The Gentleman and Cabinet Maker's Director*. Writers in Chippendale's lifetime observed nothing unusual to record regarding his activities. The few bills now remaining are written on plain paper: no example of a trade card has come to light.

The year that he first set up as a master cabinet-maker in London remains unknown, but shortly after his marriage to Catherine Redshaw in May 1748 he was established at

Conduit Court, a paved passage-way between Nos. 17 and 18 Long Acre. In mid-summer 1752 he moved to Somerset Court, Strand, recorded by Strype in 1720 as "a handsome new-built Court with houses fit for good inhabitants". Somerset Court adjoined Northumberland House and could be approached only through a covered passage-way beneath No. 2, Strand. Everything, timber and finished work alike, had of necessity to be man-handled through this passage for Somerset Court was a cul-de-sac. Canaletto's painting of Charing Cross in 1753 shows Somerset Court entrance and a row of prosperous shops extending from each side of Northumberland House. The rate books prove Thomas Chippendale to have occupied No. 1 Somerset Court until the end of 1753, and a deed of trust recorded in the Middlesex Register, 1757, states that it was "formerly in the Tenure of Thomas Chippendale at a yearly Rent of Twenty Seven Pounds".

Chippendale's premises were, then, of substantial quality, and a plan dated 1759 shows the ground area to have measured 20 feet wide and about 45 feet long, the back set against the south wall of Northumberland House. The plan shows Nos. 1 and 2 Somerset Court to have been identical. A drawing of the ground-floor front room of No. 2, preserved in the Westminister Public Library, shows a spacious, finely panelled apartment with two ceiling-high windows facing the Court, and two open doors giving glimpses into other rooms beyond. Such a set of chambers would make an admirable show-room for fine furniture. Shortly after Chippendale left Somerset Court its name was changed to Northumberland Court. This has confused some authorities into believing the two addresses to have been different premises.

Whilst trading in Somerset Court, Thomas Chippendale no doubt became acquainted with the Earl of Northumberland to whom he dedicated his *Director*. Chippendale's business obviously must have increased for in the following year he moved to the upper part of St. Martin's Lane, one of the few London streets then paved. Its residents included peers, celebrated scientists and doctors, eminent artists and rich merchants. Already three distinguished cabinet-makers were trading there: William Vile and James Cobb in partnership

23

at the corner of St. Martin's Lane and Long Acre from 1750, and William Hallett at No. 71, next door, from 1752. The Middlesex Registers, 1754, show that Chippendale acquired possession of Nos. 60 and 61, two houses separated by a covered cartway entrance passage giving access to a stable yard and workshops, the land measuring about 250 feet long and at its widest about 180 feet (*see page* 33).

In addition to organising the publication of the *Director* in 1754 Chippendale built workshops, warehouses, timber stack, and shop, all enclosed within the substantial brick or stone wall required by law for workshops storing inflammable goods. No windows or other openings were permitted in these boundary walls.

Chippendale and a financing partner, James Rannie, insured their brick and timber workshops and warehouses, Chippendale's residence at No. 60, their stock-in-trade, tools, goods-in-trust, household goods and Chippendale's clothing, with the Sun Fire Office, a firm established in 1710. Search at the Sun Insurance Office has revealed the original fire policy for £3,700 taken out by Chippendale and Rannie. The directors have kindly permitted the wording of the policy to be reproduced here:

"POLICY NO. 144850 DATED 4th FEBRUARY 1755.

FIRST PREMIUM—£8:9s:–d. ANNUAL PREMIUM—£7:9s.–d
RENEWAL DATE—LADYDAY 1756.

THOMAS CHIPPENDALE of St. Martins Lane in the Parish of St. Martins in the Fields and JAMES RANNIE of . . . Cabinetmakers and upholsterers on the now Dwelling House of the said Thomas Chippendale Situate as aforesaid with a warehouse behind adjoining and Communicating on the Right Hand Side of the yard not Exceeding Eight Hundred Pounds   £800

On their Household Goods utensils and Stock in Trade and Goods in Trust therein and under the said Warehouse and over the roof thereof not Exceeding Sixteen Hundred and Fifty pounds   1650

Glass therein only not Exceeding One Hundred pounds   100

Wearing apparel in the Dwelling house the Property
of Thomas Chippendale not Exceeding Fifty pounds   £50

On a warehouse only intended to be built at the End
of the yard to adjoin and Communicate with the
aforesaid Warehouse not Exceeding Two Hundred
and Fifty pounds   250

On their Shop only Situate On the Left Hand side
of the said yard Opposite to the first and adjoining the
Last mentioned warehouse not Exceeding One
Hundred and Fifty pounds   150

Utensils Stock in Trade and Goods in Trust Therein
only not Exceeding Two Hundred pounds   200

& On their Utensils Stock in Trade and goods in
Trust in their Back yard & in the Shops therein
adjoining Each other behind the Intended warehouse
with a Brick Wall between not Exceeding Five
Hundred pounds   500

    £3700

all Brick & Timber buildings"

A plan of Chippendale's premises was prepared at a later
date by the Sun Insurance Office. This, unfortunately, cannot now be traced, but a copy made in the 1930s by the
London County Council follows the lay-out described in the
policy. Chippendale's residence at 60 St. Martin's Lane, to
the right of the cartway, was a three-storied building of
brick and timber with cellars. Behind, on the right of the
yard and divided from the house by a built-over vestibule,
was a timber-built warehouse measuring about 150 feet long
by 30 feet wide. The floor above was roofed with boards
pitched over, and was fitted with frames for drying stacks
of timber by means of a German stove. This, with the house,
was insured for £800 and their contents for £1,750.

By the late 1760s this building had become the upholsterer's workshop with its own staff of a qualified overseer
and women assistants. The frontage facing the yard of this
and other workshops was of timber framing covered with
finishing mortar set with a row of fenestrations running the

entire length of the buildings with double sliding doors midway for the entry of goods. On the opposite side of the yard was the retail shop which with its stock was insured for £350.

At first the actual cabinet-making was carried on in a three-storied workshop built at the far end of the site, each room measuring about 60 feet by 20 feet, three sides in brick, the front and floors in timber. Chippendale was fortunate in having insured this for £500 as less than three months after he had paid the first premium the *Gentleman's Magazine* reported that it had been "consumed by fire and the chests of 22 workmen were destroyed". This was rebuilt, together with a three-storied building extending the full 180 feet width of the site and joining the shop and warehouse.

The ground floor of No. 61 St. Martin's Lane, included in the Chippendale–Rannie lease but not mentioned in the insurance policy, appears to have been converted into a showroom with display windows running the length of the entrance passage and facing the blank wall of No. 60.

Hitherto the second edition of the *Director* has been attributed to 1755. This is contradicted by an advertisement in the *London Chronicle* dated 9th March 1758. The advertisement announced:

"This Day was published
Neatly engraved on 160 Folio Copper-Plates
Price 1£ 16s. bound 2£ 2s

THE GENTLEMAN and CABINET MAKER'S DIRECTOR: Comprehending a great Variety of the most useful and elegant Designs of Household Furniture in the Gothic, Chinese, and Modern Taste; with Scales & Directions for executing the most complicated Enrichments and Decorations of each Design.
By T. CHIPPENDALE, of St. Martin's Lane, Cabinet-Maker. Printed for the Author, and sold by R. Sayer in Fleet-street.

All Commissions for Household Furniture, or Drawings thereof, sent to the Cabinet & Upholstery Warehouse, at the Chair in St. Martin's Lane, will be most punctually observed, and executed in the genteelest Taste, and on the most reasonable Terms, by the Public's most humble Servants,

T. Chippendale and J. Rannie."

The premises appear to have been unaltered until after the death of Rannie in 1766 when Chippendale sold the stock-in-trade, advertising it almost daily in the *Morning Advertiser* from 3rd to 17th March 1766 as "consisting of a great Variety of fine Mahogany and Tulip Wood, Cabinets, Desks, and Book-cases, Cloathes Presses, Double Chests of Drawers, Commodes, Buroes, fine Library, Writing, Card, Dining and other Tables, Turkey and other Carpets, one of which is 13 feet by 19 feet, fine pattern chairs, and sundry other Pieces of curious Cabinet Work, a large Parcel of fine season'd Feathers as also all large unwrought Stock consisting of fine Mahogany and other Woods, in Plank, Boards, Vanier and Wainscot." The dispersal of this huge stock of *Director*-type furniture, then fast becoming outmoded, occupied several days.

Chippendale now set himself up, not only as a cabinet-maker and upholsterer, but as a general house-furnisher. The production of fine cabinet work in mahogany continued: in addition he made inlaid (more exactly marquetry), painted and japanned furniture. The premises were reorganised and alterations made to adapt them to the new scheme. The retail shop on the left of the yard was converted into a series of workshops and included a veneering room with all its presses; a drying room with a carpet store above; a stove room for japanning; a counting house of two stories; and a small office for checking incoming and outgoing goods. The stove room was given protection of a brick frontage and a stone floor, the flue being built outside. Here was installed a newly designed japanning stove or oven measuring about 8 feet by 6 feet and probably 12 feet high, for hardening the japan under a very low, equable heat supplied by a German stove. This prevented warping or shrinking the wood.

The nearby cabinet-making block was now devoted to other purposes. The plan shows the top floor to have become a feather room containing an open radiating cockle stove for keeping the feathers thoroughly dry. There was also a small feather room above the veneering shop, and an extensive glass room where mirror plate was silvered and re-silvered.

Only when the style and scope of such premises are envisaged is it possible to understand many of the details in the few existing accounts of his supplies and services, to Nostell

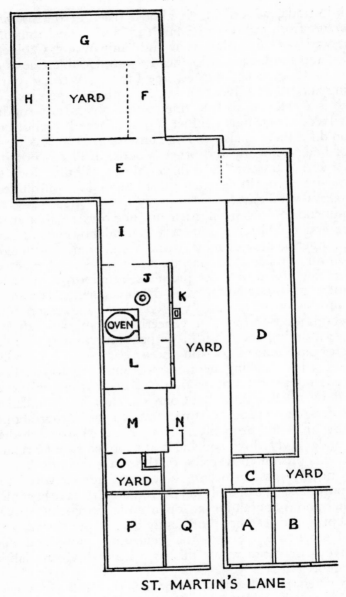

ST. MARTIN'S LANE

Fig. 1.   Thomas Chippendale's Premises

28

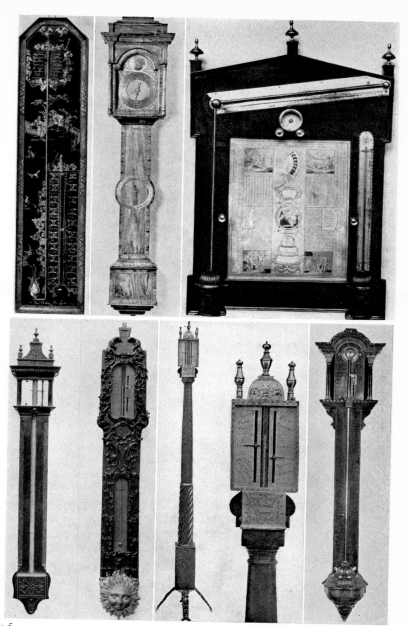

Plate 5

Barometers. (*Top left*) Siphon barometer with thermometer in a black and gold lacquer frame, by Isaac Robelon, London. Dated 1719. (*Top centre*) Rare walnut wheel barometer of the pediment type invented and made by John Halifax, Barnsley. Dated 1725. (*Top right*) Diagonal barometer and thermometer on mahogany frame enclosing a "Perpetual Calendar of Time" and a variety of attachments introduced when the calendar was revised in 1752. Made by Watkins and Smith, London. Dated 1753. (*Lower left*) Barometer with rectangular cistern and case of carved mahogany. The register plates are enamelled. 1750s. (*Lower left centre*) Carved mahogany in the rococo style, by John Ayscough. 1750s. (*Lower right centre*) Two views of a portable barometer by Daniel Quare, with silvered register dial and brass case. (*Lower right*) Torricellian barometer in mahogany frame with pediment hood, by J. Bird, London. George II's reign.

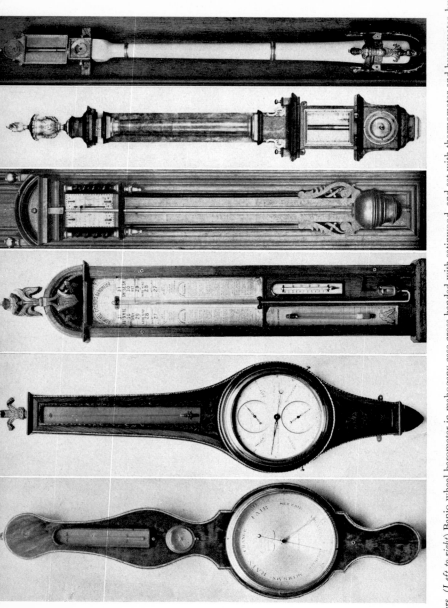

Plate 6

Barometers. (*Left to right*) Banjo wheel barometer in mahogany case cross-banded with satinwood, and set with thermometer and hygrometer, by Lione Somalvico, London. Wheel barometer in mahogany case inlaid with satinwood and edged with ormolu cordwork. Made by John Russell, Falkirk, about 1810. Admiral Fitzroy's barometer with an oak frame containing a storm glass and thermometer; 1870s. Cistern barometer with a flat burr walnut case, pediment hood and silvered brass register plates; about 1700. Syphon barometer in a burr walnut case with ormolu mounts and a manually operated calendar dial, by Thomas Tompion; 1690s. Portable barometer with turned ivory case, ormolu mounts and three hinged feet of chased gilded

Priory, Mersham Hatch and the like. The renovation of feather beds was an important part of an upholsterer's trade. In 1771 Chippendale, Haigh & Company charged David Garrick 9s. 9d. for "emptying a Feather Bed and Bolster, beating the Feathers and filling again", and "to difference in exchange of Old Mixd Feathers out of a Bed and Bolster for fine season'd Goose feathers £1.13.0". From this account and many others also specifying in detail each item of merchandise and service, it is possible to visualise the scope of Chippendale's upholstering activities, now carried out in the former warehouse on the right side of the yard. Much was repair and renovation work, such as washing the textiles that furnished a bed, making up and lengthening curtains, and making covers for chairs, calculated and billed to the last tape and tack and curtain ring. He was even prepared to undertake paperhanging and would send men to hang pictures or move furniture.

In the manner continued into present times he must have bought in a great amount of minor goods made speculatively by poor, single-family workshops in the area. If his *Director* brought him ultimate fame, much of his passing success must have been achieved by a humbler capacity to make his great establishment generally useful to the rich families in the vicinity.

George Seddon (1727–1801), the Aldersgate Street cabinet-maker, was a passionate believer in opulent display. He transformed a bishop's palace into craftsmen's workshops, and eventually into a modern house-furnishing store with extensive workshops at the rear. He became wealthy by exploiting his flair for anticipating coming fashions in furniture design, making the most of the colours and grains displayed by newly imported exotic woods, and draping his

THOMAS CHIPPENDALE'S PREMISES IN ST. MARTIN'S LANE, LONDON

A. No. 60 St. Martin's Lane: counting rooms and dwelling house.   B. No. 59 St. Martin's Lane: Chippendale occupied the ground floor of this house.   C. Three-storied building   D. Upholsterers' shop and ware room heated with a German stove. On the roof were stacks for the drying of wood. This was covered with boards and pitched over.   E. Three-storied building: ground, sheds and ware rooms; 1st floor, glass room; upper floor, feather room with an open cockle stove.   F. Open covered passage with two stories above.   G. Three-storied building: all cabinet-maker's shops.   H. Shed with room above.   I. Veneering room with feather room over.   J. Drying room with stone floor for charcoals; containing a japanning stove and German stove. Carpet room above.   K. Flue.   L. Store room and showroom.   M. Two-storied building: ground floor a counting house; storeroom above,   N. Counting house.   O. Yard.   P. No. 62 St. Martin's Lane: dwelling house   Q. No. 61 St. Martin's Lane.

showrooms with sumptuous upholstery textiles for richly appointed homes. Simultaneously, from the early 1770s, he worked on mass-production lines appealing to the middle-income public rejoicing with understandable extravagance at the development of large-scale manufacture. Every new process, every new tool was throughly investigated and if successful in action was immediately installed.

At the age of twenty-three he founded what was to become the great firm of Seddon, at London House, former home of the Bishops of London and the refuge of Princess Anne, later queen, during the revolution of 1688. This brick-built residence, enclosing a spacious paved court-yard with a lamp in the centre, was fronted on Aldersgate Street by a nine-columned portico and massive wrought-iron gates, later to be painted blue and enriched with gilding. The pine-panelled state-rooms were used to display mahogany furniture in the Chippendale style; the chapel, library, audit house and coach house became spacious workshops. Seddon insured premises, tools and stock with the Sun Fire Office for £3,300, a sum equivalent to more than £60,000 today. Its two acres of ground were enclosed within a substantial brick boundary wall.

Sir Ambrose Heal's researches have shown that George Seddon was apprenticed in 1743 to George Clemapon, Mugwell Street, Cripplegate, his father John Seddon of Blakelea, Lancashire, paying a premium of £16. The family appears to have been moneyed for George, an eighth child, to be financed in the business of a master cabinet-maker on so grand a scale immediately after completing his apprenticeship. The insurance entries refer only to George Seddon: no partnership is suggested.

The London directories make no reference to Seddon until 1763 when *Mortimer's Universal Director* printed a one-line entry: "George Seddon, Cabinet-Maker, Aldersgate Street." During the late 1760s the Aldersgate Street shop signs were removed in compliance with the statute, 2 George III, c. 21, and the property numbered, London House becoming No. 158. Fortune favoured Seddon until 1768 when his premises were entirely destroyed by fire. The extent of the fire and the havoc caused were important enough for the event to find a place in the *Annual Register* of that year where it was recorded that "a dreadful fire burnt down London House, formerly the residence of the Bishops of London, now occupied by Mr. Seddon, one of the most eminent cabinet-makers of London. He employed 80 cabinet-makers and the damage is computed at £20,000."

This figure, which is often quoted, was an over-estimate, however. The Sun Insurance Office have kindly extracted the following from the Minutes of a meeting of the Committee of Management held on 28th July 1768: "Read a Petition from George Seddon setting forth that he had been a Sufferer at the late Fire in Aldersgate Street to the amount of £7300 & upwards, of which £3300 was insur'd at this Office, but had omitted to pay his Annual Premium in proper Time, & praying the Office to take his Melancholy Case into consideration, by bestowing on him what in their kindness and compassion, they shall think proper to Grant. Order'd that several Circumstances appearing in favour of the said George Seddon, & in Consideration of his great Distress, of All Claim on the office under his Policy." Seddon's business had more than doubled in value between 1750 and 1768. Meanwhile he had neglected to increase his original coverage, and, worse still had omitted to pay his annual premium when due.

It has been thought hitherto that Seddon moved after the fire. Actually the firm always occupied the site of the original London House. Seddon built new premises on the site— which extended behind other adjoining property fronting Aldersgate Street: a plan of the period shows the property to have consisted of two shops, one of which was let. Aldersgate Street appears to have been re-numbered at this time, the new houses now being Nos. 150 and 151. Seddon retained No. 151 as the showroom of the new London House. Directory entries between 1770 and 1784 give his number as 151. Fire continued to menace Seddon and in 1783 London House, with its neighbour No. 150, was destroyed. On the double site, however, he built imposing premises consisting of cellars, semi-basement, ground floor, three upper stories and a flat roof for seasoning timber.

In 1786 Seddon took his 21-year-old younger son George

into partnership, trading as George Seddon & Son. They were joined in 1790 by Seddon's elder son Thomas, and his son-in-law Thomas Shackleton. A bill made out in 1790 has the name "and Shackleton" added in ink to the printed inscription. In the same year fire ravaged London House for the third time, Seddon's younger daughter being burned to death. In the previous two years the firm's stock had been valued at £118,926, inclusive of timber £21,702; carpets £9,064; and the contents of the upholstery warehouse £3,293.

The activities of George Seddon were vividly and comprehensively recorded by the German novelist Sophie von la Roche, who visited London House on 16th September 1786. Her diary has been translated by Clare Williams and was published in 1933 under the title *Sophie in London*. After noting that four hundred men and women were employed on the premises, she wrote of Seddon himself that "he seems to me to be a respectable man, a man of genius with an understanding for the needs of the needy [those in average circumstances] and luxurious."

No comparable description of a Georgian cabinet-maker's workshop has yet come to light, although it is obvious that Seddon was already operating as a manufactory. Sophie von la Roche observed that the furniture-making processes were carried on in a building of six wings additionally to a "sawhouse where as many logs of fine foreign wood piled, as firs and oaks are seen at our saw-mills. The entire story of the wood, as used for both inexpensive and costly furniture and the method of treating it, can be traced in this establishment."

Seddon's bills at this time were sub-headed "Cabinet-Makers and Upholders, also Manufacturers of British Cast Large Plate Glass". Sophie states that in one of the basements "mirrors were cast and cut". In this she was mistaken for glass was not made at London House: no insurance company either then or since would undertake to cover such a risk in association with combustible furniture and upholstery. The glass plates were cast at Ravenhead, St. Helens, a glasshouse established in 1773 and financed to the extent of £8,000 by David Garrick. The wording of the

Plate 7
Bird-cages. (*Top*) Oak with carved lower railing and cresting, believed to have been in the possession of Nell Gwynn in the 1670s. (*Below*) Architectural bird-cage chiefly of walnut: the top and back are closed by gilded iron bars. Eighteenth century.

3 +

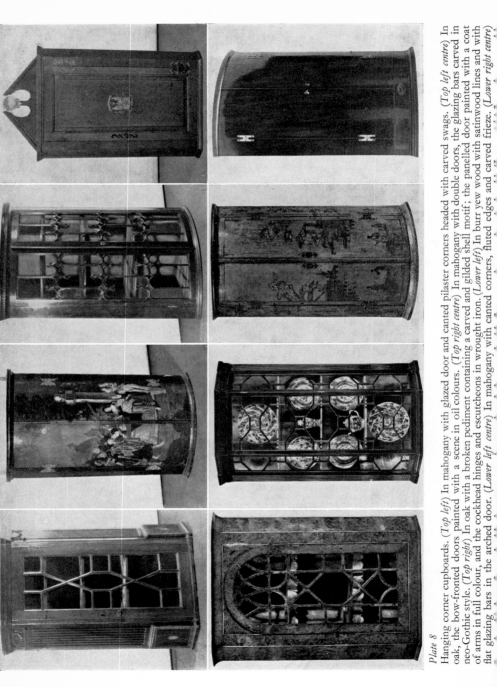

Plate 8

Hanging corner cupboards. (*Top left*) In mahogany with glazed door and canted pilaster corners headed with carved swags. (*Top left centre*) In oak, the bow-fronted doors painted with a scene in oil colours. (*Top right centre*) In mahogany with double doors, the glazing bars carved in neo-Gothic style. (*Top right*) In oak with a broken pediment containing a carved and gilded shell motif; the panelled door painted with a coat of arms in full colour, and the cockhead hinges and escutcheons in wrought iron. (*Lower left*) In burr yew wood with satinwood lines and with flat glazing bars in the arched door. (*Lower left centre*) In mahogany with canted corners, fluted edges and carved frieze. (*Lower right centre*) bill-head makes it reasonable to suggest that George Seddon was one of the eight financing partners.

Seddon's "manufacturing" consisted of fitting out a basement with machines for the flat grinding, bevelling and polishing of cast plates, received from Ravenhead in a rough state. More than one-third of all consignments of plate glass were lost through breakage during transport and the hazards of the hand-operated machines. For this reason plate glass was rarely finished at the glasshouse, but was despatched to London and elsewhere for machining. In addition to the cost of losses in transport there was an excise duty of eight shillings in the pound sterling on plate glass—hence the high cost of mirror plates. Seddon also operated a department for the highly profitable business of silvering the polished plates.

Sophie noted the tools used by Seddon's workmen and was told that they were forged in Birmingham. By supplying his turners, carvers and so on with tools forged from the improved cast steel then available, he drastically reduced the maintenance costs of continually re-shaping and re-sharpening, and work was finished more quickly and efficiently. Until suitable crucibles were invented in the early 1790s only small quantities of this steel were available, and only to selected customers. It was costly and only within the means of cabinet-makers in a big way of business.

Sophie's reference to "the girdlers who moulded the bronze into graceful patterns" shows that Seddon operated a foundry and workshop for making ormolu enrichments for furniture, hall lanterns, and such like, gilding them by the dangerous mercury method. He also made brass handles mechanically chased on a machine bought from John Pickering of Birmingham. This was really a hand-operated stamping press capable of applying ornament to soft brass, the cost of the tools making it profitable only on long runs.

Seddon's visitor from Germany was vastly impressed by the showrooms. The manager of each section would receive a guinea a week, assistants twelve to fifteen shillings.

One department observed by Sophie "contained nothing but chairs, sofas and stools of every description, some quite simple, others exquisitely carved and made of all varieties of

3*   33

wood". In adjoining showrooms were laid out "writing-tables, cupboards, chests of drawers, charmingly fashioned desks, chests, both large and small, work- and toilet-tables in all manner of wood and patterns, from the simplest and cheapest to the most elegant and expensive". A huge hall was reserved for bedroom furniture, four-posters complete with hangings and counterpanes taking up great space.

It was "the scheme of a dining room designed both for practical use and ornament" that attracted her most. "It contained a mahogany table some feet in breadth, of which a third [quarter] on either side is reserved for drawers, with an opening in the middle like most writing tables have . . . by pressing a spring where the drawers are indicated by attractive fittings, a lead-lined compartment flies open with shelves, where the wine-bottles are kept in water, with the monteith fixed on either side. There were two foot-stools [pedestals] of the same wood, and made to match, and fine dark marble vases with lids to them on the side [top]. In these foot-stools are two tiny cupboards, one lined with sheet-iron and neat grillers, on which plates can be heated by the red-hot iron beneath them; the other is meant to keep salt cellars and other table utensils. The vases up above hold spoons, knives and forks."

As a member of the Upholders' Company George Seddon dealt in furnishing textiles. Sophie expressed her interest in the department where she saw a great many seamstresses and "chintz, silk and wool materials for curtain and bed covers; hangings in every possible material; carpets and stair carpets to order; in short anything one might desire to furnish a house".

Although Seddon was responsible for an immense quantity of furniture during his half-century of active business, and thousands must remain, very few authenticated examples have come to light.

Furniture still exists, however, associated with a Seddon bill for £414 11s. 4½d. made out in 1790 to Mr. D. Tupper, Guernsey, and illustrated in Old Furniture, 1928. This includes "18 Satinwood Elbow Chairs round fronts & hollow can'd seats neatly Japanned—ornamented with roses in back and peacock feather border", cost 73s. 6d. each; "28

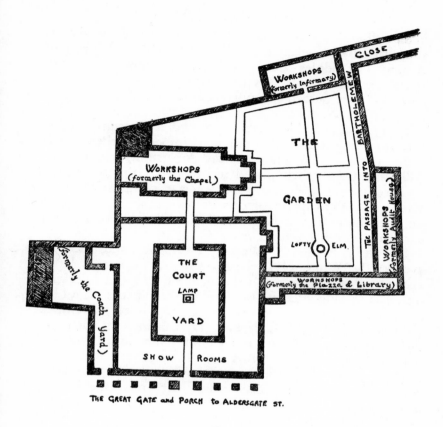

The figure is labelled as follows:

CLOSE

WORKSHOPS (formerly Infirmary)

INTO BARTHOLEMEW

THE

WORKSHOPS (formerly the Chapel)

GARDEN

WORKSHOPS (formerly Audit House)

THE PASSAGE

LOFTY O ELM

THE COURT

LAMP

YARD

WORKSHOPS (formerly the Piazza & Library)

(formerly the Coach Yard)

SHOW ROOMS

THE GREAT GATE and PORCH to ALDERSGATE ST.

Fig. 2.   Plan of London House, Aldersgate Street, former residence of the Bishops of London: acquired about 1750 by George Seddon for workshops and showrooms

Mahogany Chairs strait fronts sweep sides stuff'd & cover'd in Satten hair Cloth & finish'd with 2 rows of brass nails moulded taper feet", cost 40s. each. The satinwood chairs were fitted with cushions covered with loose cases of "rich Polampoes, lin'd & bound with white cotton Lace and fring'd with green mixed fringe Gymp head", costing 16s. 6d. each. Matching the satinwood chairs was a five-back settee for £17 10s. 0d. and three French stools at £5 15s. 6d. each. The

35

SMALL ANTIQUE FURNITURE

latter still exist and are seen to be chairs with extended seats supported by six legs. Included on the bill are "A pair of elegant Girandoles double branched ornament'd with Baskets of fruit carv'd & Gilt in burnish'd Gold, £12.0.0" and "2 Vause Screens on pillar and Claw Stands to match Chairs, £6.0.0".

In 1793 the Seddon firm exported a consignment of furniture to a wealthy Norwegian timber merchant Niels Aalls, Ulefoss Manor house, near Porsgrunn, where some still remain with their priced record of each piece and the date of payment. Their purchase was commissioned by Aalls from the captain of one of his timber ships plying between London and Norway. This priced list of English furniture was printed in *Ulefoss* (Oslo, 1940).

The list is headed "Mahogany Furniture" and prices 28 pieces: "1 White Oval Japan Mirror, £8.0.0; 1 Japan mahogany colour £4.0.0; 1 do smaller do £3.10.0; Packing 19s. 4d.: 12 Single Chairs modern White Japan with a blue Stripe, Stuffed with best Horsehair and lined with thick linen at 28/-, £16.16.0; Packing 12/-: 6 do Arm Chairs at 35/-, £10.10.0; Packing 12/-: 1 Sofa White Japan £11.0.0; 1 mahogany folding Screen 18/-; Packing 8/-: 1 mahogany Commode £5.5.0; packing 4/-: 1 White Japan Commode £5.5.0; packing 4/-: 1 mahogany Chair Commode £2.2.0; 1 mahogany Cheese Cradle 4/-; 1 mahogany Commode Mirror modern £1.14.0; packing 4/-: Expenses at the Customs House 15/8." The bill totalled £73 3s. 0d. and this amount was paid to "Mr. Seddon & Son" on the 6th June 1793.

All of these may be classed as useful furniture and typical of the bulk of Seddon production of the 1780s and 1790s. The mahogany close-stool in the form of a four-drawer commode resembles an example noted in Seddon's showrooms and described by Sophie von la Roche six years earlier. The mahogany chest of drawers with a flap opening downward to form a desk and revealing drawers and cupboards with satinwood fronts was an early example of factory-made dual-purpose furniture with brass handles of the mechanically raised type. The mahogany vase-shaped dressing-table mirror on a three-drawer pedestal and edged

36

with narrow banding in holly (Plate 4) and termed "modern" in the bill, is similar to one recorded by Sophie von la Roche in 1786, the shape matching those of so-called Hepplewhite shield-back chairs; and the chest of drawers in white japan enriched with decorations in blue well illustrates the shaped bracket legs newly introduced to factory-made furniture.

Seddon was always anxious to introduce newly designed pieces of furniture to the public. One of these was an ingenious portable combination writing-table and filing cabinet known as a croft. A leaflet, pasted within an example discovered by Sir Ambrose Heal and fully discussed by him in *Country Life*, January 1947, makes an eight-point announcement regarding its use, stating also that it was "Manufactured and sold by Messrs. Seddon, Sons & Shackleton, Aldersgate St., London".

Seddon's large-scale firm also made and marketed dual-purpose furniture patented in 1798 by Day Gunby, a carpenter of Hatton Garden. The specification included drawings of a desk with a rising section of drawers and pigeon-holes operated by cords (Plate 4). Manufacturing rights were acquired by the Seddon firm, and to each piece was screwed a brass label bearing the name Seddon with the word "Patent" above and a serial number below.

In the early 1790s came the opportunity for producing useful furniture for the less affluent on an even more expansive scale. The firm installed a series of machines for moulding, grooving, rebating, sawing and shaping outlines, all invented by Sir Samuel Bentham. The driving force was, presumably, steam, but not until about 1810 were steam-driven lathes operating in furniture factories.

Seddon's son George in the early 1790s established retail furnishing houses at No. 10 Charterhouse Street and in the Mayfair district where palaces and palatial mansions were rising on a spectacular scale, ideal recipients for the costly cabinet-made furniture of the finest woods then being made at London House. George Seddon senior died in 1801 and his sons Thomas and George became sole proprietors, continuing fine traditional craftsmanship side by side with factory methods.

37

Attribution of antique furniture to specific makers is so rare in Britain that shrewd collectors began to take an interest in the extremely enterprising firm of Morgan & Sanders. It is probable that a wider range of this firm's products will be recognised as more collectors seek out the dual-purpose articles characteristic of their "patent" manufactory.

If some of the Regency period's ingenuity in devising these dual-purpose furnishings appears misplaced it must be recognised that the new furniture factories with their revolutionary methods had sated the market for conventional designs. Even by 1800 the plain-surfaced, unenterprising furniture from these factories was in such large supply that demand was falling. Thomas Morgan and John Sanders were successful and are remembered today because they devised original and interesting furniture while making use of the factory's price-cutting, labour-saving techniques. Thus they established themselves as specialists in "patent" furniture in which two, three or even as many as seven purposes might be combined in one unit at little more than the cost of a single piece. Unlike cabinet furniture which necessarily must be crated for transport, "patent" furniture could be dismantled into sections and closely packed into flat boxes without space wastage. This drastically reduced costly wagon and shipping charges. A single pack horse might now carry a set of a dozen chairs into remote country places.

To cite an example of their methods, Morgan & Sanders appear to have foreseen potential profits in patent No. 2420 granted to John Elwick on 1st July 1800 for "framing together chairs and soffas of every kind and which invention is intended to be applied to every description of household furniture . . . and is principally useful and convenient for package and for exportation". For instance, chair legs were "tapped with either a right or left hand screw top", and joined by stretchers provided with screw ends. Seats were movable: at the back was a dovetail slide fitting into a groove cut on the inside edge of the back rail. Other designs dispensed with stretchers.

The partners either acquired sole rights in this patent or were licensed to manufacture, for their trade card, in the collection of Sir Ambrose Heal, illustrates and describes such "portable chairs, plain & with Arms, of Mahogany or elegantly Japan'd, made to any pattern, a dozen of which pack in the space of two Common chairs".

Morgan & Sanders in 1801 acquired Nos. 16 and 17 Catherine Street, three doors from the Strand, a few houses below Drury Lane Theatre. *Holden's Directory*, 1802, describes them as "upholsterers, cabinet makers and inventors of the Imperial dining tables". They remodelled the premises, installing a broad staircase of inlaid wood from the vestibule to showrooms on the first floor, extended backward to obtain overhead light. Upper floors, basements, stables and other outhouses were converted into workshops. Within five years more than one hundred men and women were employed on the premises, and by 1809 *Ackermann's Repository* estimated that full employment was also given to a thousand outworkers and that the firm had "infused new life into every department of the business of furnishing".

The firm's activities may be traced in press advertise-ments, particularly in *Ackermann's Repository* where editorial notices of their newest furniture were frequently accom-panied by engraved, hand-coloured plates, giving vivid glimpses of fashionable Regency furnishing and furniture design. They advertised in the second number and continued for nearly one hundred consecutive issues, curiously making no change in layout or copy. This monthly advertisement in small type one column wide and three inches long announced that:

"At the PATENT SOFA-BED & CHAIR-BED MANUFACTORY, Nos. 16 & 17 Catherine Street, Strand, a newly-invented patent Sideboard & Dining Table—MORGAN & SANDERS having at very considerable expense established a very large factory and also built extensive ware rooms for the purpose of exhibiting for sale a great variety of Upholstery and Cabinet Furniture, for the furnishing of houses: a great part of which are articles perfectly *new* in principles, extremely fashionable, and universally approved of . . . in particular the Patent Sideboards and Dining Tables, combined in one piece of Furniture; the Imperial Dining Tables and Portable Chairs; the Patent Four-post and Tent Bedsteads, and especially the much admired Sofa Beds and Chair Beds."

The trade card issued by Morgan & Sanders might more reasonably be considered a leaflet. Engraved by T. Alldridge,

Helmet Court, Strand, it measures about 12 inches by 8 inches and illustrates fourteen examples of furniture and a flamboyant headpiece including the royal arms. The engravings show the imperial dining table open and closed; three portable chairs with typical Sheraton square backs (they subscribed to Sheraton's *Cabinet Dictionary*, 1803) and an upholstered sofa bed which is shown as a sofa and also when transformed by simple manipulations in less than a minute into a double four-post bedstead with hangings and bedding. Three sketches demonstrate an upholstered chair and its conversion into a tent bed. A footnote announces: "A very convenient and highly approved SOFA BED, contrived on purpose for Captain's Cabins, & Ladies or Gentlemen, going to the EAST or WEST INDIES, with every other Article necessary for Voyages and use of Foreign Climates: Musquito Nett Furniture, Beddings &c."

The imperial dining table upon which Morgan & Sanders founded their prosperity had a few straight legs instead of the period's inconvenient pillar and four-claw arrangements, would open or close to seat many or few diners, and could easily be dismantled and packed into a shallow box. When Lord Nelson was furnishing Merton in 1805 he commissioned such a table in mahogany with a matching sideboard, so designed that the table when closed could be pushed into the heart of the sideboard and the loose leaves stored in a compartment above, masked by a falling front simulating a drawer. This sideboard complete with its table of seven leaves and ten legs is now in the Nelson Museum, Portsmouth. After Nelson's death Morgan & Sanders marketed this combined sideboard-table under the name of "The Trafalgar Patent Sideboard".

Early in 1808 Morgan & Sanders acquired or licensed rights in a patent (No. 3090, December 1807) granted to George Remington, for a globe table. They adapted this to form a combined terrestrial globe and writing desk, naming it "Pitt's Cabinet Globe Writing Table". This was described and illustrated with three hand-coloured engravings in *Ackermann's Repository*, Vol. 3. At first sight this appeared to be merely a 26-inch terrestrial globe supported on a four-clawed pedestal of mahogany with a wide horizon circle.

Pressure upon a plain ball finial operated a patent lock containing a barrel spring and pulley, causing the two upper quarters of the globe to slide downward into the lower hemisphere, revealing a circular leather-covered writing table. Renewed pressure upon the finial caused the rear interior quarter to rise, bringing with it drawers and pigeon holes. The fourth quarter was covered by a lift-up hinged lid.

This idea was adapted to ladies' work tables, the exterior of the globe being in finely figured mahogany veneer inlaid with signs of the zodiac in hollywood. Queen Charlotte bought one as a birthday gift to the Princess Augusta in 1810: it is in the possession of H.M. the Queen at Buckingham Palace. The globe is supported on three deeply convex legs of square section with gilded feet rising from a low triangular plinth and terminating in bearded masks of ormolu. When open it discloses a small temple backed by mirrors and fitted with columns of parquet flooring with numerous small drawers and receptacles for work.

The colour plates in *Ackermann's Repository* make it possible to attribute other furniture to Morgan & Sanders, such as the "ladies backgammon table with seven uses", described as "an elegant and ornamental piece for drawing room or boudoir, a convenient reading and writing table with ink and pens. By sliding the desk off, it then forms a backgammon and tric-trac table, with a chess and draught board below. Underneath hangs a handsome silk bag for a work-bag or any purpose. It is made of fashionable Brazil wood, inlaid with brass."

The "Imperial Turkey Ottoman or Circular Sofa" illustrated in the same volume was designed to "fit a bow window or room with a circular end". It closely resembles television seats of today. The frame might be in zebra-wood, kingwood, rosewood or mahogany, inlaid and ornamented with brass, ormolu or bronze. Each end might be carved from the solid wood in the form of a swan and gilded.

George III was greatly interested in the ingenious furniture evolved by Morgan & Sanders, and from time to time commanded Thomas Morgan, the technical expert in the partnership, to display newly devised examples at Buckingham Palace for the inspection of himself, the queen

41

and the princesses. This is noted on their trade card, printed before early 1806 when they named their premises Trafalgar House.

Interior decoration was numbered among their activities. In 1815 they designed and furnished a bedroom in light rosewood, reaching the height of efficiency by illuminating with four-globe gas chandeliers, with mirrors discreetly placed to increase light by reflection. The bed, mirrored back and front, fitted into a mirrored recess—a style revived during the 1950s and hailed as entirely modern. As an alternative to mirror-work Morgan & Sanders suggested quilted drapery.

A library chair in Trinity College, Oxford, bears a brass label upon which Morgan & Sanders describe themselves as "carpenters and manufacturers", indicating rightly that their factory-made productions were not classed as cabinet work. Inspection of *Repository* engravings, the firm's trade card and a few authenticated examples show that furniture of their own manufacture was in fact constructed from factory-made units. Their showrooms, however, displayed much fine cabinet work commissioned from outside sources. The demand for dual-purpose furniture continued unabated until 1815, when T. Martin wrote to *The Circle of the Mechanical Arts* that it was "the fashion of the day to resort to a number of contrivances for making one piece of furniture serve many purposes".

The Napoleonic wars assisted in bringing prosperity to Morgan & Sanders. They advertised themselves as "Makers of Army and Navy Equipage" and were government contractors as well as suppliers of furniture to officers. They were an unqualified success in devising ships' cabin furniture capable of performing a multitude of duties within a confined space, yet displaying a fashionable drawing-room appearance. Army officers and their wives recognised the firm as experts in camp beds constructed from lightweight woods.

Mahogany dressing chests for officers' wives were in constant demand, so designed that what was apparently no more than a plain travelling chest could within a few moments be transformed into an attractive and lavishly fitted piece of domestic furniture. Morgan & Sanders from about 1810 marketed a toilet dressing-case described as "a machine in which a large mirror rises from the back of the case and may be adjusted to height, distance or angle. To each side is affixed a mirror, adjustable, enabling the lady to observe her face and profiles." Drawers were divided into compartments and provided with the usual toilet requisites. A deep drawer in front formed a writing table.

Military chests for use on active service were made in mahogany, teak, camphor-wood, rosewood and oak. The design usually consisted of four drawers divided horizontally into two portable sections with D-handles on the sides for lifting. The centre of the top drawer was fitted as a secretaire with a leather-covered fall-front forming a writing table. The brass drawer handles were sunk flush into the wood to avoid projecting parts.

Factory-made war-time furniture was apparently the mainstay of the business during the few years preceding the peace of 1815. Fashionable Londoners back in their homes once again demanded fine cabinet-made furniture in colourful woods in contrast to the plain-surfaced austerity to which they had become accustomed.

Morgan & Sanders participated in the boom for costly furniture until shortly after the death of Sanders in 1818. Morgan then extended Trafalgar House to include No. 15 adjoining and traded as Morgan & Company. The demand for "patent" furniture was not revived, however, and in 1822 the business closed.

We are grateful to Dr. Ada Polak, Deputy Curator in Britain, the Arts and Crafts Museums of Norway, for drawing our attention to the Seddon furniture in Ulefoss Manor House Collection, near Porsgrunn, Norway, illustrated on Plate 4.

Chapter Three

MURAL barometers were the triumph of English scientists in the later seventeenth century and the delight of the wealthy intelligentsia throughout the eighteenth century. Magnificently framed in the succession of beautiful woods associated with the finest craftsmanship of their day, a collection presents a handsome display as well as a fascinating record of men's attempts to come to terms with their climate.

The basic truth from which the barometer tube evolved derives from Galileo's notes found after his death in 1641. This was the hitherto unobserved fact that a column of water in a pipe could not be raised higher than about 33 feet, even by creating a vacuum above it with a suction pump.

This point was seized upon by Evangelista Torricelli, a Florentine scientist who acted for some months as assistant to the blind Galileo. He soon found that the weight of the column of water varied in relation to atmospheric pressure. He then substituted mercury, fourteen times heavier than water, and proportionately reduced the scale of his experiments. With a vacuum tube, sealed at the top, he thereupon demonstrated that the height to which mercury would rise up the tube was governed by atmospheric pressure.

At the foundation meeting of the Royal Society in 1660 Robert Boyle exhibited a Torricelli tube of transparent glass to which he had fitted register plates in such a way that they showed the movement of the mercury and hence the changes of atmospheric pressure on the exposed cistern or tank of mercury at its base. This was the world's first practical barometer. Within ten years English scientists had evolved four different types of barometer: cistern, syphon, wheel and diagonal.

Sir Samuel Morland, Master of Mechanics to Charles II, evolved the cistern barometer. A 34-inch glass tube was filled with air-free mercury and its open end immersed in a small cistern of mercury. The pressure of the atmosphere on the mercury in the cistern maintained the column of mercury at a corresponding height. Tube and cistern were mounted on a wooden frame fitted with a register plate engraved with a scale of variation from 28 to 31 inches. The syphon barometer quickly followed. This had a J-shaped tube, the shorter limb exposed to the air and usually expanded into a cistern.

The wheel barometer was adapted from the syphon by Dr. Robert Hooke and illustrated in his *Micrography*, 1665. In this a float with a thread attached rested on the surface of the mercury. As this rose and fell it operated an indicator hand around a graduated dial, the inches being converted and magnified. Sir Samuel Morland in 1670 devised the diagonal barometer, known also as the "sign-post" or "yard-arm". The slightest variation in air pressure caused considerable movement of the mercury along the slanting arm and provided more accurate reading.

So far the barometer was primarily a laboratory instrument. The tube was drawn from a flimsy soda glass, soon broken by the weight of the mercury within if subject to careless usage. In 1674 George Ravenscroft patented a tough, crystal-clear flint-glass that could be drawn into long tubes of $\frac{1}{10}$-inch bore, strong enough to contain mercury without danger of fracture. But under continual temperature variations such a tube might collapse and replacements were frequent until the late 1740s when flint-glass tubes could be toughened by passing twice through the newly invented tunnel annealing lehr.

The presence of microscopic bubbles of air in the mercury tended to cause inaccuracies in reading, for these bubbles eventually rose to the top, below the vacuum, to depress the column. With the introduction of double-annealed flint-glass tubes Charles Orme of Ashby-de-la-Zouch discovered that air could be completely excluded by boiling the tube containing the mercury. Even so, filling the

45

tube with mercury was a skilled operation if the metal was to remain entirely free from air bubbles. It was essential, too, for accurate reading that barometer tubes should be of adequate bore, about $\frac{1}{10}$ inch. Some makers sacrificed accuracy in an effort to economise in expensive mercury by using tubes of smaller bore.

Lord Keeper Guilford was obviously aware of Ravenscroft's patent in 1674 and its potentialities. He then designed an elegant barometer incorporating a flint-glass mercury tube that was suitable for domestic or public use. This he commissioned from Henry Jones, a clockmaker of the Temple, who eventually became renowned as a maker of fine-quality barometers.

John Smith in his book on the *Use and Right Managing of the Barascope or Quicksilver Weatherglass*, 1688, made no reference to the term barometer. He emphasised the necessity of protecting the tube of mercury by embedding it in wood, "but for Ornament sake the Choicest are generally made use of, such as Ebony, Walnut, or Olive-Wood. . . . Near the bottom of the frame is to be affixed the Cistern-Box and a Cover of such Size and Bigness as may admit a Glass Cistern of three inches in diameter and one inch in height at Leest. Lastly upon the upper part of the frame are to be affixed the two Register-Plates, in doing which you must observe a due Distance between the Lowest Division on the Registers, and the Bottom of the Cistern-Box." Smith supplied instructions to the last detail, even to the extent of describing how the nail should be inserted into the wall for the safe hanging of the instrument.

The narrow stick or pillar barometer, about 40 inches in length, was made unceasingly for the next two centuries. Barometers were made by clockmakers and naturally frames were designed and made by those cabinet-makers then employed for making clock cases. At first the panels were for the most part flat, chosen from wood displaying attractive grain or enriched with colourful marquetry and bordered by thin raised rims, sometimes gilded. Cornice and superstructure were designed as miniatures of those decorating long-case clocks, the flanking pillars at first being of the barley-twist variety, then fluted columns, and, later, turned

46

Doric columns. At first the superstructure was placed above the register plates. By 1690 it was customary for the plates to be framed within the hood in the same way as clock dials, and similarly enriched with brass mounts, usually gilded. Metalwork on all barometers was heavily gilded to avoid polishing, essential with other metals, which at the hands of inexperienced servants might shake the column of mercury and incorporate air bubbles. At the lower end of the frame was a cistern cover plainly turned and hollowed, with a downward pointing finial. The sides of the panel, immediately above the cistern, were ornamented with a pair of scrollwork wings which might be carved or fretted. This feature is seldom found on eighteenth-century barometers.

There was little change in barometer design during the early eighteenth century, but by 1740 frames were usually of mahogany. The finest of these displayed wide panels lavishly carved in the rococo style. Throughout the second half of the eighteenth century fashionable barometer cases were designed to harmonise with changing fashion moods. The majority, however, were severely plain, broadened at head and base with a broken cornice pediment. In the 1770s and 1780s a carved oval patera might cover the cistern, the register plates being framed with matching carving within a similar oval.

From about 1800 the stick tended to become narrower, the mercury tube was concealed by a convex mahogany cover, and the register plates were enclosed by glass. The cistern was no longer open, and, although not portable, barometers might be moved gently without hazarding the mercury. By 1810 a flattish hinged box tended to supersede the turned cistern cover.

The rectangular register plate, at first of silvered brass, was divided into two sections by the mercury tube. The inner edges were engraved with degrees of atmospheric pressure ranging from 28 to 31 inches, each inch divided into twentieths. Each was flanked with lettered descriptions reading from "Dry Serene" at the top to "Rainy Stormy" below. It was also inscribed "Rising, Fair or Frost" and "Falling, Rain, Snow or Wind". In some examples a pair of knobs rising from the finial could be rotated to regulate a

47

pair of pointers on the scales. From the mid-eighteenth-century scale plates might be of white enamel with inscriptions in black: by 1810 details might be printed on highly glazed paper and pasted in position.

Portable barometers date from 1695 when Daniel Quare, the celebrated clockmaker of Exchange Alley, Cornhill, was granted a patent. This was described in the *London Gazette* on August 5th as "a Portable Barometer or Weather Glass which may be turned upside down without spoiling the Quick-silver . . . the Royal Society highly approves of it and has caused it to be entered into their Bookes as the first they had seen". Quare's invention took advantage of the fact that it was not essential for the surface of the mercury to to be exposed for it to be subject to atmospheric pressure. When it was required to move or clean the barometer, a soft leather pad, operated by a screwed rod, sealed the glass tube, thus preventing air bubbles from entering the quicksilver.

The tube of mercury was enclosed within a tapering column of ivory, ebony, walnut or japanned beech enriched with gilded ornament. The base might be square or bludgeon-shaped, and might have spiral turning immediately above. It was fitted with three hinged legs cut from latten plate, each with an ornamental casting brazed to its outer surface. The column was surmounted by a flat register plate, its pediment richly engraved with foliated scrolls. The whole of this metalwork was treble gilded. The legs were discarded from about 1710 and the portable barometer became a furnishing accessory for the wall.

Diagonal barometers reached their peak of popularity between about 1720 and the 1740s. The wooden frame was composed of two 30-inch sections: one vertical, the other extending horizontally from the top. The mercury tube rose from a cistern up the vertical limb and continued diagonally across the horizontal arm against a metal register-plate 3 inches deep, engraved with the usual details.

The vertical arm in early examples was a turned column of walnut with the mercury tube inside it: the lower portion might be twist-turned with vertical flutes above. The arm was flat and at the angle was fitted a manually operated dial for giving comparative readings. More frequently,

Plate 9
Dumb-waiters in mahogany. (*Top left*) With turned baluster stem and plain tripod foot. (*Top right*) Three tiers, showing stems cut with twisted gadroons and tray rims turned with tooled mouldings; about 1770. (*Lower left*) Two tiers with carved stem and reeded tripod. (*Lower right*) Two tiers with spindled galleries encircling the trays; about 1770.

Plate 10

Dumb-waiters in mahogany. (*Top left*) The lowest tray revolves on the pillar, the upper two being supported by turned uprights. (*Top centre*) A two-tier specimen revolving on its pillar. (*Top right*) Two tiers, with folding trays. The claws have a dipping line. Early nineteenth century. (*Lower left*) Four tiers with smooth vase-shaped stem units. The strengthening soles to the pad feet are clearly seen with the wide brass-wheeled castors below. (*Lower centre*) A three-tier example showing stem swelling with twisted gadrooning, the tray rim turned with simple tooled moulding. (*Lower right*) Two tiers with reeded column and claws in a single flowing curve; the lower tray has raised rings for dishes.

however, the frame was veneered in plain, flat burr walnut with a turned cistern cover. The favoured design from about 1730, at first in walnut, then in mahogany, was in plainly architectural lines, occasionally with a mask centrepiece and ribbon and rosette moulding.

A diagonal barometer from the early years of the eighteenth century might be incorporated in the framing of a looking-glass. This might have an imposing pediment decked with gilded brass figures in the round. Such a mirror is illustrated in an advertisement issued in 1708 by John Patrick, a celebrated maker of barometers and other meteorological instruments. Symmetry was retained by fitting a thermometer to the right member of the mirror frame. From 1753, instead of a mirror, the central area might be fitted with a printed perpetual calendar displaying information based on the revision of the calendar in 1752.

Wheel barometers were costly and infrequent until the 1760s although examples exist signed by most of the celebrated clockmakers. A series dating between 1720 and 1750 closely resemble miniature long-case clocks with heavy pediments. At first they were in finely figured walnut, then in mahogany. The square register plate possessed spandrels, and degrees of atmospheric pressure were engraved on a silvered double circle. The indicators registering mercury movement were shaped and pierced to resemble clock hands. In the arch above was a dial for giving comparative readings.

George III, who assembled a small collection of up-to-date weather instruments, made the banjo wheel barometer fashionable. This might have as many as three subsidiary register plates: a thermometer and a hygrometer, both detachable for independent use, and at the bottom a spirit level. A convex mirror might be inserted into the centre of the case. Banjo barometers in mahogany inlaid with shell or star designs and edged with stringing were made in considerable numbers. The Regency wheel barometer was usually displayed in a case of rosewood veneer cross-banded with woods in contrasting colours and inset with mother-of-pearl or brass.

The wheel barometer from the early 1820s reverted to the mount consisting of a narrow panel of mahogany with an

4+

expansive circular register plate, fitted with a vernier scale which gave a far more accurate reading than had formerly been possible. The plate was of silvered brass, with an ivory-headed actuating key, and was protected by a highly convex glass framed within a cast bezel of burnished brass. The cistern was provided with a visible ivory float for indicating zero level.

The expensive mercury barometer met with competition from 1844 when M. Vidi invented the compact and portable aneroid barometer. Its plain circular body had no need of an attractive case such as would make demands on creative craftsmanship. Although a little less accurate than the mercury barometer, this instrument is satisfactory for domestic use. The aneroid barometer is actuated by atmospheric pressure upon a shallow metallic chamber, nearly exhausted of air, with upper and lower surfaces corrugated in concentric circles and one flexible side. The short arm of a lever is kept pressed upon the elastic side and a longer arm operates an index pointer. When the atmospheric pressure increases, the box is partially crushed in; when it lessens, the elastic side recovers its shape, the index pointer moving in the opposite direction. The actual movement is very slight, but the pointer indicates it multiplied 657 times. Such barometers were advertised at £3 each in 1847.

Eventually the aneroid barometer almost displaced the mercury barometer for domestic use. One notable competitor, however, was registered at the Patent Office on 8th August 1881 and examples bear the diamond-shaped registration mark. This was Admiral Fitzroy's mercury barometer, sold at a low price hitherto believed impossible. It was made on mass-production lines and found its way into tens of thousands of homes. The flat frame was machine-shaped from imported oak and the mercury tube fully visible. A closely printed register plate gave comprehensive "remarks" for forecasting the weather from natural observations. A storm-glass containing crystals in a solution occupied one-quarter of the frame. Fitzroy kept his storm-glass formula secret, but it was based on the unreliable pre-Torricellian weather-glass.

Chapter Four

BIRD-CAGES

ENGLISH noblemen for centuries collected exotic birds with bright plumage from abroad, while in the apartments of their wives hung gilded cages gay with the voice and movement of songbirds. White nightingales and turtle doves ranked with popinjays—the early name for parrots—in value, but the women were content with such native songsters as goldfinches, larks, siskins and linnets. Great interest was also taken in talking birds such as crows, jays and magpies which were caged as household pets. The Earl of Derby's expenses for 1392 record the purchase of a new cage for the popinjay, and Maundey in about 1400 noted "pyes and papeiayes with-iune a cage". A century later exotic birds were permitted to fly unrestrained about the house. Sir Thomas More kept never fewer than a dozen uncaged popinjays, but a cage of songsters swung from the ceiling of every daytime apartment.

Times that tolerated all manner of human slavery and serfdom were unlikely to comprehend the fundamental cruelty of caging wild birds, and fortunately today's collector need be no bird fancier to find in the cages themselves fascinating reflections of what charmed and diverted leisured folk of past generations. Bird-cages have a three-thousand-year history in Europe, at first in wicker and from the eighth century B.C. in iron. An early Christian sarcophagus removed from the Vatican cemetery has carved into the stonework a domed bird-cage, a bird with outstretched wings on top signifying that the soul of the entombed person had been liberated from its earthly prison. The same theme is sculptured into the wall behind the monument to

Sir John Suckling and his wife in St. Andrew's Church, Norwich, dating to about 1630. This depicts a cage square on plan with a domed wire top and each side strengthened by a cross-piece of flat splats.

Cage birds, their cages, trappings and food are mentioned from time to time in royal inventories of the fifteenth and sixteenth centuries. Edward IV, who reigned from 1461 to 1483, possessed several resplendent popinjays and his queen hung a cage of white nightingales in her apartments. Woodcuts of the period show the cages to have been tall and square with domed tops, and suspended from the ceiling by means of pulley and cord, the latter usually coloured and enriched with gold wire. Covers, sometimes of costly fabric, might shade the cages at night: less pretentiously the covers were of a gay green cloth.

There were singing cages and silent cages: in the former the perches were set high to encourage the birds to sing; in the latter they were low. Normally the cage hung low on the cord so that the bird's colourful beauty could be seen by all: when it was required to sing, the cage was hauled close to the ceiling whereupon the occupant, if in good health, would quickly burst into song. It was customary to cover the floor of the cage with a piece of green turf which was changed frequently. Webster refers to this in the *Duchess of Malfi*, 1614: "Did'st thou ever see a lark in a cage? Such is the soul in the body; this world is like her little turf of grass."

So far but one bird-cage of the fifteenth century is known to remain, its design resembling examples illustrated in contemporary miniatures and illuminated MSS. This wrought-iron cage, discovered near Avignon and now in the Metropolitan Museum of Art, New York, is typical of those which hung lantern-like from the ceilings of English castles and manor houses until the early Stuart period. They were really stout decorative frames into which could be slipped loose cages containing birds: these could be removed so that a succession of decorative singing birds might be at the owner's disposal.

These frames were rectangular or square on plan with upright corner-posts wrought square or turned into baluster

Plate 11
Dummy-boards. (*Top left and right*) Figures of women, 5 feet high, in costumes of the early seventeenth century. The woman at her toilet was formerly at East Sutton Park, Kent. (*Below*) Interior of the Chelsea Bun-house showing three dummy-board figures above the door.

Plate 12
Dummy-boards. (*Top left*) A pedlar of the early nineteenth century. (*Top right*) A gentleman in full-bottom wig and costume of the 1690s: height 6 feet 2 inches. (*Lower left*) Young man in fashionable costume of about 1745: height 4 feet 4 inches. (*Lower right*) A figure of a maidservant peeling an apple.

and knop forms and each terminating either in a spire finial which might be topped with a tiny ball, or in a turned vase-shaped finial. These were joined at their lower ends by four pierced wrought-iron railings, 2 to 3 inches in height; a second lighter railing joined the top ends below the finials. From this a domed top, with a swivel ring at the apex, swung open on a pair of hinges. The wrought iron, a highly expensive metal at that period, was gilded by the French method of close plating. Octagonal cages were also made. Food and water jars were attached in much the same manner as to modern cages, but were of horn.

Bird-cages of silver and silver-gilt were known at the court of Elizabeth I, the lower rail sometimes being lavishly set with English pearls, Bristol diamonds, and Derbyshire gem-stones. Sometimes these cages would contain two or three brilliantly coloured birds from the orient, not alive but stuffed with sweet perfume, and with rubies for eyes. This brought about the vogue for a lighter single-piece bird-cage and they began to be made in a greater variety of patterns than formerly. Some of these are recorded in the seventeenth-century paintings by Jan Steen and Vermeer, prototypes of English patterns.

Charles II was the most prominent bird fancier of his day, Bird Cage Walk, St. James's Park remaining as a reminder of his pastime. The cages were planned by the celebrated gardener Le Notre. The king's collection of birds was kept in a series of enclosed aviaries needing a considerable staff to care for them— even a cormorant keeper at 17s. 6d. a week. Edward Stisted, page of the bedchamber, was also appointed clerk of the aviary, and in 1663 Richard Smith was appointed volary-keeper, a volary being a large bird-cage. In 1684 Edward Story was appointed volary-keeper. Nell Gwyn is reported to have delighted in her collection of white sparrows—actually, of course, canaries. In January 1661 Pepys noted in his *Diary* the delivery of two cages which "I bought this evening for my canary birds".

Bird-cages by now were being made entirely of wood with bars of iron wire, but the lantern type in metal continued to be made. As the drawing-room became more and more a fashionable necessity the bird-cage was made of oak

53

or walnut to match the furniture. The deep rail encircling the floor of the cage might be carved to harmonise with the furniture and a crest was applied resembling those on chair backs. Uprights and cross-pieces were twist-turned.

The popular bird-cage at this period was given a semi-circular bow at one end, an arrangement permitting it to extend out of an open window when placed on a suitable table. This enabled the birds to be exposed occasionally to the elements, treatment considered beneficial to their health, since some parrots, for instance, would only bathe in the rain.

Bird-cages in the eighteenth century became more numerous: the inventory of Dyrham Park taken in 1710 refers to three bird-cages in the great hall and a large cage in the ante-hall. In the great hall of Deanery Hall, Wolverhampton, there were no fewer than fifteen architectural bird-cages in the 1790s, all of which were later acquired by James Cartwright the celebrated toymaker. In addition to the work of professional bird-cage makers some were made by specialist cabinet-makers, mostly following Dutch designs of the previous century. Some of the more handsome examples were designed by architects for their clients who expected them also to supervise construction. This brought about the vogue, which lasted a full century and a half, for wooden bird-cages with the outward form of country mansions. In addition, in those days when some homely occupation was essential to fill in the long hours of evening, it was not uncommon for them to be constructed as a hobby, just as dolls' houses were.

Many bird-cages were made for standing on tables of matching wood, but the majority were of the lantern type. The floor was a loose slide which could be pulled out for cleaning. Feeders and water jars might be attached as today: in other instances lead-lined drawers were provided for this purpose. More ornamental designs had food and water jars standing upon pendant brackets screwed to the lower rail. Glasses for seeds and drinking water were consistently advertised throughout the eighteenth century. The *Post Man*, 12th February 1706, advertised: "The so much approved and most convenient new fashion Cristol Bird Glasses,

54

which effectually prevent the littering of the seeds into the the room. Made by the author T. Meyer at the Bird Cage in Long Acre."

Early in the eighteenth century there was a vogue for rectangular cages with oak corner uprights turned in the form of a series of balusters: from the square boss joining each pair extended horizontal bars of wood with brass wirework used as a filling. Formerly brass wirework had been drawn metal: now it might consist of short slender cast rods, turned and burnished.

There was usually a brass lifting handle on top resembling those on lantern clocks and four scroll or ball-and-claw feet for standing. The two-compartment decorative cage appears to date from this period, usually rectangular with a flat top, sometimes with a raised centre of wheel-spoke construction, the central oval being fitted with a swivel loop for lifting. Such cages were also made in mahogany during the second quarter of the century.

The cabinet-makers of Chippendale's day produced many highly decorative bird-cages in mahogany in a variety of styles, both of the lantern type and for resting on stands. Some examples incorporated fretwork, lattice-work and finials copied from drawings of Indian masonry: others bore some resemblance to Chinese pagodas. The purely architectural bird-cage became fashionable again from about 1760—although the demand had never really ceased—in the form of a pseudo-gothic box with a wired bow front. Two or three narrow gothic-shaped glazed windows ran the full length of each side and such cages might be japanned. Others resembled nothing so much as magnificent dolls' houses, double-fronted and with wirework at the rear.

From this period especially the most usual bird-cage was of the lantern variety designed either for standing upon a table or for hanging from the ceiling at any required height. The lower part might now be in the form of a box with turned upper and lower finials at each corner and with four drawers for food and water. The open part of the cage consisted of drawn brass bars shaped into a dome supporting a decorative platform which held the swivel ring by which the cage could be hauled to the ceiling. Ball-and-claw feet were frequent at this period.

By the 1770s the lantern-shaped cage, often on a matching stand, might have mahogany railings inlaid with shells and, like the uprights, banded with boxwood. Vase-shaped finials and turned feet were of bone or ivory. A food box in mahogany was screwed to one of the railings and fitted with a side drawer for easy replenishment. Other cages were made to fit closely into the galleries of the stands and a wide three-sectioned cage fitted with trellis wirework was made, the central section being fitted with a door. Most remaining examples have been converted into cabinets. Some of the lantern cages incorporating light-coloured wood, such as satinwood, were fitted with bars of cane instead of metal.

From about 1800 lantern bird-cages might be square and examples are known in ebony and ivory with turned ivory or gilded bars. Others had deep railings of tortoiseshell and mother-of-pearl. Sheffield-plate examples are illustrated in a pattern book at the Victoria and Albert Museum. Towards the middle of the century glass barred bird-cages appeared with woodwork painted white and the lower railing edged with ornamental ormolu and spear points of cut glass in alternating colours of red, blue, green and white.

Bird-cages in the form of houses continued to be made, some of them in Tunbridge ware. John Hull of Oldham built bird-cages in which the front took the form of the Oldham coat of arms, and one of the sides a representation of the Sailors' Home, Liverpool. The veneer was composed of 2,522 pieces of twenty-one different kinds of wood. Charles Dickie of Dundee sold ornamental bird-cages of mahogany in the form of elaborate rectangular double-domed buildings. Collectors should note that during the 1850s and 1860s James Quin of Kidderminister was making reproductions of eighteenth-century gothic bird-cages in mahogany. At this time, too, appeared a second series of ornamental lantern bird-cages with gilded bars and railings of pearl or tortoiseshell: the finest of these bear the name of H. W. Whitaker, 20 Charlotte Street, London.

Less expensively the lantern-shaped parrot and song-bird

cages were made throughout in brass which might be gilded or lacquered in blue or brown. Conical and rectangular bird-cages in wicker or basketwork for less pretentious homes were made throughout the period, but none appears to remain.

Chapter Five

CORNER CUPBOARDS

DESERVEDLY, hanging corner cupboards are among the most popular of small furniture antiques. Yet in their heyday they played a very minor role in fashionable furnishing. Trade catalogues published by the now celebrated cabinet-makers and designers feature them not at all. Customarily they were hung on living-room or parlour walls on thick hand-wrought iron nails passing through holes drilled in the back-boards.

A parlour in the eighteenth century was defined as "a lower room [ground floor] for the entertainment of the company", and it is easy to imagine how valuable they would prove, with their solid, all-concealing doors to close over the small everyday necessities, in a period when built-in cupboards were a rich man's luxury and when it was highly desirable to keep cupboards and their contents off the floor. In date their manufacture extended from the early 1700s to the 1830s, yet they remained within a comparatively small range of designs. They were treated with the inexpensive simplicity to be expected of everyday furniture yet in a notable variety of woods and finishes, including oak, walnut, mahogany, fruit woods, tulip-wood, pine and japanned and painted effects. They form an entirely different group from the glazed hanging cupboards used in formal rooms for the display of fine porcelains and more properly classified as cabinets.

Not until the 1760s were these unpretentious pieces made in quantity. With their plain cornices rising about a couple of inches above the cupboard top, they were obviously designed to hang above eye level. Here the mistress of a

58

middle-class home might store her newly acquired table services of the enamelled cream-coloured earthenware then superseding smithum-glazed pottery, pewter and wood. In a country home the boarded top might be used to display a row of glass ale flutes each containing a colourful Easter egg.

Provincial manufacture continued in the early nineteenth-century, many of these crude cupboards obviously being the work of carpenters. Two pictures painted in London by Sir David Wilkie, R.A., between 1805 and 1810 illustrate corner cupboards in comfortable well-to-do homes. In "The Card Players", the scene is laid in a living-room kitchen: an open door provides a glimpse into the parlour where there is a mahogany corner cupboard, its convex single door enriched with a pair of butterfly hinges in brass and a diamond-shaped keyhole escutcheon in ivory or bone.

Wilkie's "Rent Day" records the interior of a dining-living-room in a late eighteenth-century mansion. The master receives his rents amid a scene of luxurious refresh-ment. High in one corner hangs the cupboard with its four-plank single door wide open to reveal three shelves. The top shelf holds a porcelain toddy bowl, drinking glasses and a square decanter; the lower shelves and floor of the cupboard are filled with a silver tea-set; and on the flat top of the cupboard stand two parchment-covered jars of pickles and a wanded flask.

Late seventeenth-century cabinet-makers were already designing hanging cupboards. The front frame and door of such a cupboard were in fine cabinet wood, the rest of the cupboard in some lighter, easily worked wood such as deal. Fashionably the cupboard front was in walnut veneer until this was outmoded by mahogany about half a century later. Straight doors were characteristic at first, with lines of herringbone pattern to suggest panel effects. But the fashions of the early eighteenth century soon demanded a hooded cornice, its dome boarded in from the top. This was fitted with an arch-headed or semicircular door with a cupid-bow panel of veneered burr walnut in well-balanced figure to give symmetrical, uniform patterns. The door was boarded with straight-grained strips. In a few examples it was panelled with an arch-headed bevel-edged mirror. Some cupboards were designed with straight cornices and the sides might be fluted pilasters: later came the swan-neck pediment. When double doors were used the line of the join was covered with a length of plain moulding, often semicircular.

Such cabinet-makers' corner cupboards were comparative rarities. More at this period belonged to the special class of furniture in which entirely simple outline and cheap material adequately served to display a gleaming japanned ground enriched with decorations in gold. The ground colour might be black, cream, green or red, a mock tortoise-shell ground being fashionable during the middle years of the century. This formed the background for all-over pictures composed mainly of Chinese motifs in gold and colours such as figures on terraces with buildings, garden landscapes and scenic water.

These often sold in matching pairs, although Lady Grisell Baillie recorded in her household account book of 1715 that she paid ten shillings for a single japanned corner cupboard. By that time the flat top of such a cupboard might be surmounted by a series of two or three small open corner shelves of convex or undulating outline for displaying ornaments. Three shelves inside the cupboard were concealed by single or double convex doors.

The rich effects of japanning may have prompted the introduction of painting in oil colours that eventually became a feature of hanging corner cupboards constructed in oak or deal. Floral patterns against light-hued grounds such as ivory or the palest of warm greens were favourites. A pair with panelled doors has been noted, one painted with exotic birds and fruit, and the other with a vase of flowers. Flower groups adapted from contemporary botanical illustrations might be surrounded by small posies in the style featured by porcelain painters. Watteauesque figures in garden landscapes were fashionable on panelled doors during the third quarter of the eighteenth century.

The interiors of japanned and painted corner cupboards were brightened with coloured paints in various hues of red, green, yellow and the favourite sky blue. Door interiors, particularly the double convex type, might be additionally decorated, figures in gold on a green ground having a long

Plate 13

Heraldic panel in paper filigree showing the royal arms as borne by George I.

Plate 14
Filigree paper work. (*Top*) Hexagonal tea-caddy with embroidered panel. About 1800.
(*Below*) An extremely elaborate setting of paper filigree work around a child portrait in wax.
The floral wreath, flower vases, birds and framework contain a notably wide range of rolled
paper forms. Signed with a monogram and the date 1702.

vogue. Scenic panels might also be painted on door interiors: an example recently noted displayed four scenes from the story of Susannah and the Elders.

Hinges on walnut, japanned and painted corner cupboards were five-lugged and almost invariably of brass, the cock's head and associated patterns being most frequent. Keyhole escutcheons were rectangular of shaped outline, often with fleur-de-lis upper and lower finials. A dummy escutcheon might appear on the left convex door of a japanned or painted cupboard. At first hinges and escutcheons were engraved with flowers and foliage in matching sets: later they were saw-pierced. They were secured to the wood by brass rivets, ten or twelve to each hinge, two or four to the escutcheon plates.

As was to be expected of such pleasantly homely furniture, some of the most attractive early Georgian specimens are in oak. These might be hooded or crested with carved pediments, the arch-head doors following the fashion set by long-case clocks. The cornice moulding was convex, the base moulding concave with its lower edge extending outward. These cupboards had straight fronts extending from wall to wall. When their style changed in the later eighteenth century it was in direct imitation of the most typical of best-loved corner cupboards in mahogany.

Mahogany hanging corner cupboards in quantity date only from the 1760s onwards and even then for a short time they continued the styles familiar in walnut. Then splay corners were introduced and these might be vertically fluted or decorated with lattice-work either carved from the solid or in the form of applied fretwork. The arch of the door panel might contain applied fret ornament somewhat after the style of contemporary street door leaded fanlights. This was but a transitional style, however, and by the 1780s flat effects of inlay and marquetry had superseded fretwork surface ornament.

The pediment continued as an almost constant feature in finer examples, the most frequent forms being the broken arch and the swan-neck with graceful scrolls set wide apart, flanking the central lower pedestal that supported the brass urn, torch, ball and spike, or other ornamental finial.

Slender scroll pediments might contain elaborate lattice work.

The majority of hanging mahogany corner cupboards, however, were straight-topped with a cornice of dentil or plain moulding. Double doors were more frequent than formerly, particularly when the front was convex. These were usually of solid mahogany, each door 12 inches wide, being built from three 4-inch planks suitable curved and fitted together with tongue and groove. Richly figured veneers were used on a base of pine, including satinwood and tulip-wood as well as mahogany. The panel effect was achieved with lines of stringing or small geometrical motifs and checker borders, and with bands of holly, ebony, or other contrasting woods. Medallion ornament such as paterae, stars and shells might decorate veneered doors. The stiles flanking the door might be fluted in pilaster form and extend from base to cornice, sometimes picked out in gilding. By the mid-1780s wide pilaster ornament was replaced with narrower cheeks having splay sides that might be plain, panelled or fluted.

Brass hinges served as the highlights on the rich brown of less decorated mahogany. The cock's head outlines and pierced hinges continued, and H-hinges were common. In some instances inconspicuous butt hinges were introduced, two or three to each door and screwed. Provincial examples in oak might have three-lug butterfly hinges in wrought iron. Shelves were uniformly straight or curved; their rounded edges might be gilt and their surfaces grooved to support plates. Interiors were usually painted in dull red or pale green.

Factory furniture-makers from the late 1780s made doors for corner cupboards by the thousand. Many of these, easily packed for transport, were sold to London and provincial cabinet-makers who provided the rest of the cupboard with its shelves in deal, and who fitted hinges, lock and keyhole escutcheons.

Most Regency period doors were plain and solid: the straight-fronted were panelled and usually single, the bow-fronted might have either single or double doors according to their width. Panels on convex doors might be suggested by the use of crossbanding with narrow lines of stringing, dark and light. From about 1790 a length of reeding might cover the join of double doors and from about 1810 this might be in brass. The majority of these late corner cupboards had flat, plainly moulded cornices with sometimes a row of simple pear-drops arcades below the mould, but the hooded pediments with vase finials of earlier years were still made by provincial cabinet-makers. Fitted beneath or inside the cupboard might be two or three shallow drawers with knobs which might be repeated on the doors. Knobs might be screwed to the doors of earlier cupboards at this period. Fruit-wood corner cupboards have been noted, their doors inlaid with vari-coloured flowers and with three graduated shelves above three more below.

Oak cupboards of the 1760s onwards introduced the same splay-sided design at first with a hooded or pediment top, then with a carved dentil cornice and moulded base, or with moulding for both cornice and base. The single or double doors were plainly panelled with moulded borders. Splayed sides at this period might be decorated with lattice work, either carved or applied. Convex doors in oak were also made. Some oak corner cupboards were inlaid unpretentiously with native fruit-woods in borders, scrolls and shells, reflecting the taste of the period.

Examination of a large collection of hanging corner cupboards showed how little variety there was in size or proportions. Among about a hundred specimens the width ranged only from 19 inches to 24 inches, about half measuring 22 inches; interior depth from 15 inches to 18 inches; height from 30 inches to 50 inches. Only in two provincial oak examples did width exceed height.

Chapter Six

SWEETMEAT and fruit banquets served in the drawing-room were fashionable social entertainments throughout the Georgian era. Glass pyramids, each composed of two, three or four stemmed waiters, piled one upon the other in gradually diminishing sizes, were loaded with wet and dry confections in their appropriate glasses. Bedecked with posies, these would stand in colourful magnificence down the middle of a table completely enveloped with spotless hand-woven calendered damask and spread with dishes of fruits, plates knives and napkins. Instead of being seated, the guests might converse as they stood or strolled about the room in the manner of a modern cocktail party. Wines were served by waiters or goblet boys, each carrying a stemmed glass waiter laden with drinking-glasses and a bottle or flask of wine.

This considerable group of servants wandering among the guests made private conversation virtually impossible: it was well-known that waiters conspired to sell any overheard secrets or indiscretions to quarters where such information might have cash value. Letitia Pilkington in her *Diary*, 1758, tells of personal servants whose real profession was black-mail, their positions in private service obtained solely for this purpose.

This nuisance was lessened in the 1730s by the introduction of the mahogany dumb-waiter, described by Sheraton three-quarters of century later as "a useful piece of furniture to serve in some respects the place of a waiter, whence it was so named". This piece of furniture was a purely English innovation which took almost forty years to reach the Continent.

Plate 15

Cheval fire-screens. (*Top left*) Carved and gilt, containing a panel of Beauvais tapestry; late eighteenth century. (*Top right*) Walnut with baluster stretcher and original needlework. (*Lower left*) Mahogany frame carved with wave pattern and milling, mounted with original embroidery of the Rape of Proserpine; 1740s. (*Lower right*) Pinewood carved with rococo ornament and gilded, containing a panel of petit-point needlework. This resembles Chippendale's designs for "Horse Fire-Screens" illustrated in the *Director*, 1754.

Plate 16
(*Top left*) Walnut games table with two flaps, one for cards, the other for tea. Within the frieze is a tric-trac board. The legs swing back to support the flaps. Early eighteenth century. (*Top right*) Mahogany games table with two flaps and drawers to contain games accessories. Mid-eighteenth century. (*Lower left*) Games table in amboyna wood, with a single drawer and a slide below for chess on one side and backgammon on the reverse. The top opens, turning on a swivel to form a card table with a central panel of green leather. Early nineteenth century. (*Below right*) Combined games, reading and work table, the top section in burr yew, the lower in straight-grained yew.

Ralph Edwards in *The Dictionary of English Furniture* notes that the *Avant Coureur*, 25th February 1771, refers to the dumb-waiter as an English invention only then spread to France. The dumb-waiter was the cabinet-maker's interpretation of the glass pyramid, and consisted of three or four circular trays of gradually diminishing sizes revolving on a central stem based on a pillar-and-claw fitted with castors. In height it might measure about 3½ feet to 5 feet, the lowest tray between 24 and 30 inches in diameter.

The earliest reference to a dumb-waiter so far noted is in the will of Frances, Lady Colepeper, dated 1738: "I give unto my said niece . . . my dumb-waiter and the rest of my waiters." Ralph Edwards has noted that Benjamin Goodison, royal cabinet-maker 1740–1767, who made walnut and mahogany furniture for the royal palaces, supplied to Kensington Palace in 1750 "two mahogany Dumb Waiters on Castors" at a cost of two guineas each.

Dumb-waiters were soon found to be convenient for everyday service in the home. Captain P. Drake was sufficiently impressed by the introduction of a dumb-waiter into the room during one of his visits to consider it worth recording in his memoirs 1755: "As soon as supper was over, Glasses and a Bottle of Burgundy, with a Flask of Champaigne, was laid on the Table, with a supply of those Wines on a Dumb-Waiter."

Dumb-waiters loaded with cakes and caudle were placed in the waiting-room at St. James's Palace during each of the few days preceding the birth of the Prince of Wales, later George IV, in August 1762. This was the customary refreshment extended to all who called to offer their congratulations on such occasions. Each day the visitors consumed £100 worth of cakes and eight gallons of caudle.

The use of dumb-waiters for the service of dessert on informal occasions was noted by James Boswell in 1779: "We dined in all the elegance of two courses and a dessert with dumb-waiters."

Other diarists recorded the introduction of informal dining-room arrangements in which a pair of dumb-waiters were wheeled in by servants and placed at diagonal corners of the table enabling master and mistress to have at hand

5*

those meal-time accessories normally found on the sideboard, thus dispensing with the presence of servants.

Dumb-waiters may be divided into two groups: those made by cabinet-makers and the more frequent examples made by wood-turners. Early examples were made individually from the finest mahogany by highly skilled craftsmen working from drawings prepared by master cabinet-makers. The stem was composed of three or four sturdy vase-shaped or inverted baluster sections elaborately carved and made to fit tightly into each other with just sufficient clearance between each to enable the tray to revolve smoothly and without rocking. Their ends, which withstood friction of the tray, were of large diameter. The top tray was strengthened beneath with a wooden flange measuring about one-third the tray's diameter: this permitted the spindle around which the tray revolved to be of adequate length without the necessity of drilling through the tray. The lowest stem section fitted into the substantially turned and carved pillar below, supported by three legs terminating in claw-and-ball feet.

These costly pieces of furniture find no place in the illustrated catalogues of Chippendale (1754) or Ince and Mayhew (1759–1763) for by then the wood-turners experienced in tray turning were producing a less flamboyant version at considerably lower cost, individuality giving place to small-scale mass production in mahogany of a less expensive quality. In the collection of Sir Ambrose Heal is a trade card issued in about 1755 by Thomas Hollinshed, turner, corner of Great Queen Street, Drury Lane, London, announcing that he made "all sorts of Turnery Goods in Mahogany, Wallnut tree &c . . . Viz. Dumb Waiters, Claw Tables, Fire Screens, Tea Kettle Stands, Candlestands, Shades and Screens, Trays and Tea Boards in the newest Fashion".

Trays were cut by specialist craftsmen operating lathes designed for the purpose and powered by wheelboys. Each was turned from a single piece of mahogany of substantial thickness to prevent warping. It was sunk with a shallow depression, curving gracefully down from the edge into the flat surface of the tray. The edge was usually encircled with a carved repetitive motif such as tiny leaves or beads. As

66

planks of mahogany measuring two feet and more in width became scarce and costly, a lower tray would often be constructed from two pieces of mahogany almost invisibly joined. Trays were stained and upper surfaces given a hard, smooth, laborious polish known as "teaboardy" to the tray turners.

From the middle of the century until the 1790s cabinet-makers produced but a few dumb-waiters and when they did the essential units were bought from specialist turners who possessed the necessary equipment for the speedy production of trays, stem sections and pillar-and-claw with widely spreading pad feet. Consequently little carved work is found although throughout the period the knees of the claw might receive shallow ornament, frequently in acanthus design. Diminutive castors were almost invisible beneath the expansive feet. Until about 1770 castors were of solid leather.

The turners' version of the dumb-waiter displayed no decoration other than could be turned on a pole lathe. The stem sections were in vase form with the upper part fluted and the lower bulge gadrooned. By 1760 stem sections were turned in graduated sizes, the set of three or four being so designed that the central stem of a dumb-waiter tapered gracefully in harmony with the cone effect given by the trays. From the late 1760s the fluting might be omitted from the upper portions of the stem sections which remained plain, the swellings being lathe-cut with twisted gadrooning. By the mid-1770s the gadrooning too might be omitted, giving the vase-shaped stems the unencumbered smoothness approved at this period.

The pillar and claws were so shaped with boldly up-curved knees that the terminating pad feet rested flat upon the floor. Each foot was strengthened beneath by the addition of a thick sole placed with its grain running in the reverse direction to that of the foot, which otherwise tended to split when a castor was attached.

The only other opportunity for ornament was on the narrow rim around each tray. The inner edge of such a rim now rose vertically from the flat surface of the tray but the exterior edge sloped outward, its surface sometimes decorated

67

with simple tooled moulding. From the early 1780s the rim might have a vertical outer edge encircled with a single deep incision, the upper and lower edges being rounded off. The incision might be centrally placed, but more usually was nearer to the tray surface, and its width varied. Candle-slides might swing out from beneath the centre tray and a pair of deep oval receptacles also turned from mahogany, probably for finger bowls, might be fitted into the lowest tray near to the outer rim and diametrically opposite to each other. Spindle galleries encircled some dumb-waiter trays from the late 1750s; others had lattice or other perforated galleries of mahogany.

Two trade cards in the collection of Sir Ambrose Heal illustrate three-tier dumb-waiters of types being made in about 1770. The trade card of William Russell, a mahogany turner with a shop in Bond's Stables and living in Fetter Lane, London, shows an example galleried with alternate oval and circular piercing, plainly turned cylindrical stems, and with plain knees and pad feet to the pillar claw. Francis Pigner, in business at George Yard, Lombard Street, London, from 1765 to 1792, illustrates a pad-footed dumb-waiter with sharply tapering stem. As Pigner announced himself on this card as successor to Mr. Powle, it is reasonable to assume that the copper plate was engraved in the late 1760s.

As in other claw furniture, the later years of the eighteenth century showed a tendency towards slender, less vigorous designs. Especially, the claws themselves lost the double curve that had conveyed a sense of gripping the floor and now assumed a single flowing curve, sometimes an arch but more often a dipping line. Such legs, square in section, might be given fashionable reeded ornament: the broader the reeding the later the piece. Similar reeding encircled the vertical edges of the trays which from 1800 might be flat-surfaced without upstanding rims. Each foot was now fitted with a slightly tapering square-socket swivel castor of cast brass. This had horns and wheel extending beyond its plain socket which, until about 1820, was fixed rigidly and permanently into position without the aid of screws. Claw castors with wheels swivelling directly below the horizontal sockets appeared in about 1800 and five years later the upper surface and end might be cast with fluting in deep relief, matching that on the leg itself.

From the 1780s two-tier dumb-waiters were also made, measuring about three feet in height and consequently more suitable as dining-table accessories than the taller examples. Early specimens are merely three-tier dumb-waiters lacking the top section, with paw feet and with their trays sometimes encircled by spindle galleries. Like a few of the three-tier variety, occasional examples are found in which an urn-shaped finial of turned mahogany rises from the centre of the upper tray. This facilitates adjustments of the trays if either becomes loose on its spindle and tends to rock.

By the 1790s dumb-waiters were used in dining-rooms to their virtual exclusion elsewhere. Design was elaborated and the work once again was undertaken mainly by cabinet-makers. Thomas Sheraton in his *Cabinet Dictionary*, 1803, comments that dumb-waiters were then invariably of mahogany and intended for use in the dining parlour. He illustrates a two-tier example with the claw in the form of four dipping legs. The lower tray is encircled beneath with several drawers for silver and cutlery, the upper surface suitably galleried for two piles of plates, decanters and wine bottles: the upper tier, encircled with a low pierced brass gallery, is shown with pedestal-stemmed wine-glasses.

Sheraton also illustrates a horse-shoe table, at which guests would be seated at the outer perimeter and served from the inner side, with a three-tier dumb-waiter standing in the centre. This has a four-legged claw supporting a baluster shaped block below the trays and the graduated stem sections above are in the same design. The lowest tray is edged with a high fretted gallery spaced in four equidistant sections allowing easy access to dessert plates. The second tier with a low encircling fretted gallery is for wine-glasses; from the centre of the top tray rises a three-branch candelabrum.

Regency cabinet-makers constructed a three-tier dumb-waiter with rectangular trays of graduated sizes fitted to a one-piece tapering octagonal stem rising from a low four-leg claw with a reeded central pillar. The box-like lowest tray

69

contained two drawers extending from each of the narrow ends, with a pair of light holders swinging out from beneath; the second tray was also fitted with drawers while the uppermost folded with hinged flaps.

The war-time shortage of mahogany during the Regency period, especially as regards the already rare planks measuring two feet and more in width, prompted cabinet-makers to make two- and three-tier dumb-waiters with folding trays, enabling them to use narrower, thinner, less expensive planks. The hinged flaps of each tray hung down from the sides of a narrow centre-piece through which the stem unit fitted, permitting the tray to revolve. When the flaps were lifted and held in position by wing brackets they formed a flat-surfaced rimless tray, the wood being too thin for depressions to be turned. Such dumb-waiters found a subsidiary use as fire-screens. In most instances care was taken to employ attractively grained mahogany.

A new and ugly type of dumb-waiter was introduced early in the nineteenth century by the turners. This dispensed with the sturdy central stem and consisted of a pillar-and-claw table with a revolving top from which rose three slender colonnettes or turned uprights to support the middle tier, and above that again three more colonnettes for the third tier. In some instances these uprights were of cast brass and the trays encircled with pierced brass galleries. From about 1820 there might be four colonnettes instead of three and all the trays were of equal diameter.

Dumb-waiters continued in use during early Victorian days, the majority being turners' productions. Thackeray and Dickens mentioned them frequently. In *Vanity Fair* for instance reference is made to an "old-fashioned crabbed knife-box on a dumb-waiter".

Chapter Seven

DUMMY-BOARD FIGURES

ENGLISHMEN with their time-honoured love of open
fires have always turned to the hearth for colour and
warmth and good company. But when the ashes were grey
and even the fire-irons put away for the summer, the dark
emptiness of the fireplace was correspondingly melancholy.
For nearly two centuries lively dummy-board figures
offered a colourful summer substitute for the winter fires.
As such they earned the common name of fire-screen, to
the confusion of those collectors who imagine they once
endangered their wooden backs and glossy paint beside the
flames. But, in any case, the name is too restrictive for
figures that invaded every quarter of the house and gardens
during their eighteenth-century heyday and remain in some
numbers today as a frank or delightful commentary on the
period that produced them.

The frontispiece to the *Compleat Gamester*, 1674, shows a
card-playing party with a dummy-board of a fashionably
dressed man standing before a fireplace, his feet wide apart,
and in his hand a baluster-stemmed drinking glass held by its
foot in the manner of the period.

A dummy-board at that time was a heavy object, 5–6 feet
in height, cut from oak or pitch pine 1½ inches thick and
feather-edged, with a block support enabling it to stand
independently. But even then it was entirely unsuitable as a
screen against the heat of the fire for the wood must have
warped, the planks opened, and the oil-paint flaked away
under the heat of the seventeenth-century fires. So success-
fully did they enliven the empty hearth, however, that by early
Georgian days dummy-board figures, life-size but cut from

71

much thinner wood than formerly, were used for decoration and amusement all about the house. A resplendently painted soldier might stand at attention on each side of the porch; the entrance hall might become fashionably bucolic by the introduction of a peasant and a milkmaid, perhaps, in the idyllic manner of two figures in porcelain, or a shepherd and shepherdess, sometimes with sheep; good-looking house-maids gave life to dreary passages or stood on staircase bends; and romping children might be found in all sorts of unexpected corners.

The figure stood at floor level. A projecting ledge extending from shoulder to shoulder at the back kept it 6 inches from the wall and attached to it by means of a pair of wrought-iron hooks and staples. This position and the feather edges caused a life-like shadow to be thrown against the wall, aiding the three-dimensional effect. Careful place-ment was essential for the figure might be painted full-face or three-quarter face, rarely in profile. In an alcove, such as at a stair bend, the figure was kept erect by means of a pair of wooden supports cut in the shape of feet projecting 4 or 5 inches to the front, and with heels projecting to the rear. Holes in existing examples show them to have been screwed down from the heels.

Life-size soldiers in the uniform worn by Grenadiers of the Second Regiment of Foot during the reign of George I must have been particularly striking when their gorgeous uniforms appeared in the full radiance of unfaded paint. These approximate 7 feet in height, their mitre-shaped hats being about 18 inches high. They are always found with their feet 18 inches apart, then the attitude of attention: the "heels together" position dates from the time of the Prussian influence on the English army in the mid-eighteenth century.

An engraving of the interior of the Old Chelsea Bun House (Plate 11) illustrates a pair of Grenadiers and an equestrian dummy-board, displayed on brackets above the doorway, each throwing a shadow on the wall. Pairs consisting of a Grenadier and a housemaid have been recorded.

The so-called housemaids were apparently a stock pattern, a number of which still remain, identical in shape and pose, measuring 5 feet in height, but dressed differently. These maids wear white or baize aprons and are shown sweeping with soft bristle brooms of a standard pattern with the hairs fixed to a round stock with three ornamental knops above. These figures appear to represent ladies rather than house-maids—worthy housewives participating laudably if not very onerously in the domestic chores. Because of their dress housemaid dummy-boards are attributed to the 1630s, but a century later is a more reasonable date, dress and pose having been copied from an earlier source. Dummy-board figures dressed in the style of a century earlier—examples painted in Elizabethan attire are known—might have been intended for early Georgian humorists to perpetrate jokes upon the imaginative, convincing them that they had been face to face with a ghost.

Inventory references to dummy-board figures are rare. *The Dictionary of English Furniture* (Country Life, 1954) notes such an entry in the inventory, dated 1710, of furniture in the ante-hall of Mr. Blathwayt's house, Dyrham: "a woman payring of an apple". An example at Knole shows such a woman in servant's dress. In the Earl of Derby's collection is a pair of ladies, one wearing a towering head-dress in a style known as the commode or fontange, an early eighteenth-century fashion. Other early Georgian figures, of which several examples have been recorded, include a lady at her toilet, holding a mirror and brushing her hair (Plate 11); ballad singers and knights in armour.

A third group of picture-board dummies date from late in George II's reign until the 1790s. These measured between 3 and 4 feet in height and were used to enliven hearth interiors during the summer months when the burnished steel portable grate, fender and fire irons, all requiring daily attention to retain their mirror-like brilliancy, were oiled and laid away until the chilly September evenings necessi-tated their return. The chimney was closed and the space made colourful with expansive ornaments. Conversation pieces of the period show such ornament as tall lidded urns in gaudily enamelled porcelain, huge jars displaying an abundance of flowers or leaf branches, and terrestrial globes.

Dummy-board representations of these, too, might be

used, particularly of large urns displaying colourful flowers. Alternatively the entire fireplace opening might be masked by a fireboard covered with textile or paper harmonising with the wall decoration, or painted with jars of flowers or other ornament. *The Dictionary of English Furniture* refers to the Tapestry Room at Osterly containing a fireboard covered with tapestry worked as a basket of flowers and that "in the Etruscan Room in the same house was a fireboard painted in the same style, for which Robert Adam's design is preserved in the Soane Museum".

The fireplace recess, however, plain-surfaced and cleaned of its soot, proved an attractive setting for dummy-board figures, or these might be additional to a papered fireboard background. Such figures were usually presented in matching pairs of brilliantly costumed boys and girls, the boys often riding stick hobby-horses. These might stand upon elaborately carved plinths of mahogany or gilded beech, but in most instances their lower edge was set into a weighty block of oak about 5 inches thick, japanned red.

The final phase of dummy-board furniture, dating from the 1780s, was comprehensively described by Mr. H. Syer Cuming in *The Journal of the Archeological Association*, 1875. "Pleasure grounds were embellished, and dwelling houses decked with mimic life and mimic furniture. . . . I have seen a fictitious punch-bowl painted so true to nature that when placed on a bracket above a door it might well pass with nine out of every ten persons for the genuine 17th century porcelain ware of China. . . . I well remember a tabby cat which looked like life when placed in the corner of a room. The dogs were sometimes frightfully real, appearing ready to fly at any intruder when intended to occupy a place in the hall or near a gate, but when the deceit was designed for the parlour the dog wore a friendly aspect. The macaws and parrots exhibited their due variety of bright tints, and passed for the real things when stood on a high shelf or lofty perch." Cuming also refers to the late-Georgian fashion of placing red-coated soldiers on guard in tea gardens and pleasure grounds, naming such resorts as Jenny's Whim, near Chelsea; the Red House, Battersea; the Green Man, Old Kent Road; the Montpelier Gardens, Walworth.

These figures were all life-size and in outdoor positions were so arranged that visitors would confront them suddenly and might believe that they were facing realities. Sailors, standing or dancing the hornpipe, were favourites in the gardens of waterside taverns. Soldiers in a variety of red-coated uniforms still guarded mansion porches and were popular ornaments on hotel stair-cases and at tavern door-ways. Favourites with landlords of country inns were tempting picture-board dummies of jugs and glasses, dishes of onions and radishes and bread and cheese. Pedlars and women hawkers were favourite outdoor figures. Kilted Highlanders were frequent, such dummy-boards standing at the doors of tobacco and snuff shops.

Reproductions of eighteenth-century dummy-board figures were made in the 1870s and again during the 1920s, the latter often portraits copied from well-known paintings and standing with the aid of hinged brackets as on an easel.

The wooden slabs—known as tables—upon which the images were painted were at first in oak or pitch pine: in the eighteenth century beech, pearwood and mahogany were frequent alternatives. Those intended for outdoor ornament were cut from 1-inch teak, a heavy timber neither warping nor shrinking under the stress of changing weather conditions.

Outlines were cut at first from single boards of oak measuring about 2 feet wide and 1½ inches thick. The majority, however, were built up from 12-inch planks. In the early eighteenth century their usual thickness was about 1 inch, later reduced to half that amount. The edges were feathered, that is bevelled widely and sharply at the back. The tables for dummy-boards measuring between 3 and 4 feet in height were between ¼-inch and ⅜-inch in thickness.

The planks on most existing seventeenth- and eighteenth-century dummy-boards have shrunk slightly revealing the vertical tongue-and-groove joints. The Victoria and Albert Museum example catalogued as "Young man in fashionable costume of about 1745: height 4 ft. 4 inches, width 2 ft. 6 inches" (Plate 12) has so shrunk that the table is seen to consist of many jointed sections. For instance, there is a joint on the right arm shoulder, another at the elbow, and one across the hand. This potential defect was known to their makers for some dummy-boards were canvas covered, the fabric glued to a table ¾-inch thick and feather-edged. The back might also be coated with canvas and painted brown.

Dummy-board figures were the work of shop-sign painters with studios for the most part in Harp Alley, Shoe Lane. They were a numerous group of inferior artists working in open-fronted premises where sign-boards and dummy-boards might be viewed. Dummy-board pictures became less costly ornaments from the late 1760s when the demand for sign painters diminished and competition became fierce. This followed the enforcement of the 1762 statute making it illegal to suspend a sign-board over the highway. This brought about the removal of thousands of sign-boards in London and sign painters were without employment. The existence of identical dummy-board pictures, of undoubted eighteenth-century origin and cut from a single template, proves their commercial origin.

Until this time professional artists might be called upon to paint dummy-boards. These are recognised by their life-like pose and vivacious facial expressions: it is thought that many of them were portraits.

The artist or sign-painter first drew his outline upon a smooth-surfaced board built from seasoned wood. This was sawn to shape and the edges sharply bevelled. Two or three washes of boiling linseed oil were then applied followed by a rubbing down with distemper or powdered white lead mixed with parchment paste. The oil colours were painted over this, the distemper soaking up excess oil and thus giving greater brilliance to the paint. This radiance was enhanced on fine work by burnishing, particularly effective on gold and reds. The final result was varnished.

Chapter Eight

NARROW strips of parchment, vellum, even paper, rolled in spirals and scrolls and edge-glued to a flat surface, can present patterns formed by their exposed edges which remarkably resemble metal filigree. Whenever such costly wire work has been in favour there has been a tendency for its charms to be reflected in this dainty paper substitute. In pre-Reformation days it was associated with church decorations; in its later revivals it constituted a young lady's accomplishment, but one that was taken seriously enough to support paid instructors and to have left the present-day collector a fascinating assortment of highly decorative panels, tea-caddies, and even larger pieces of furniture.

Such scrolls of parchment and vellum, gilded and painted in bright colours and enriched with beads and threads of gold or silver-gilt, were used in English churches and religious houses during the fifteenth century and until the Reformation. Here they simulated the intricate magnificence of gold filigree work which formed a radiant background for ecclesiastical sculptures.

Paper filigree work, known to collectors as rolled-paper work, was revived as a minor secular art after the restoration of the monarchy in 1660 until about 1715, and again between 1775 and 1810. In these two later periods it was usual to introduce tiny rolls of paper placed on edge and pasted closely together as a background to the main pattern. This was executed in more varied scrolls, curves and loops of parchment, vellum, or stiff paper similarly edge-attached and gilded on the edge that was displayed. Thus the design shows in gold filigree against a light background.

The technique of rolled-paper work was simple. Parchment, vellum, or hand-made paper, all naturally creamy coloured and in various thicknesses, were cut into narrow strips, usually slightly more than one-eighth of an inch wide. For the background these were rolled into tight cylinders, each a closely compact roll of material. Other strips were crimped or shaped into required motifs such as close and open spirals, scrolls, loops, volutes, cones. A design was built up from these which might be copied from a pattern sold specially for this purpose.

The displayed edges might be left in their original tints or coloured, but the majority were heavily gilded and burnished. This gilding on parchment or vellum might produce a result so closely approximating gold wire filigree work that experts have been deceived into describing examples as metalwork. When edges were left untouched the finished effect resembles carved ivory or boxwood. The worker in this medium, therefore, may produce a monochrome filigree suggestive of fine chip carving or a glowing polychrome mosaic, further enriched by a multi-coloured background.

The rolled strips were glued to a base of wood covered with silk or paper. Many examples of the period 1660–1715 were in the form of panels framed and glazed for wall decoration in a day when pictures were few and expensive, but small furniture included boxes and mirror frames. Examples display a free use of cone-shaped and other projecting motifs, and the background rolls, most frequently of parchment or vellum, were usually in their natural colour and slightly irregular of surface, the finished effect resembling carved wood.

Much of this early work is religious, heraldic, or purely formal in design, and very often follows the contemporaneous vogue for decorative wrought-iron or brass work enclosing a composition of *cuir bouilli*. Stiff strips of parchment manipulated into gilded scroll work might surround a medallion depicting a religious emblem, the Passion Cross being a favourite. This was constructed from scrolls of coloured flowers and garlands. Other seventeenth-century

78

centres included painted miniatures, carved cameos, and portraits in wax. Just as the period's elaborate miniature frames were lavishly jewelled, so seed pearls, small shells, and metal threads might be incorporated into the paper-filigree decoration, in such details as the costume of small wax figures. Paper filigree heraldic work of this period is noted for the exquisite workmanship and vivid colouring.

In the Lady Lever Art Gallery there is a framed panel representing Queen Anne (Frontispiece). Her bust, arms and hands are of wax, but the intricate elaboration of her costume and the draped curtain background are composed of tiny rolls and scrolls of gilded and coloured paper. Another panel in the same collection, dated 1702, displays a wax bust of a young girl surrounded by coloured and gilded scroll work (Plate 14).

Like the raised work embroideries and other late seventeenth-century pastimes, filigree paper work appears to have gone out of fashion early in the eighteenth century, but it was revived in the mid-1770s. It was now primarily an occupation for ladies of leisure, although practised and taught by professionals who also finished work, specialising in framed panels. In filigree paper work of this period the rolled paper was regular and perfectly flat. When the original colours and gilding have remained clean, protected with glazing against more than a century and a half of dust, the effect is daintily brilliant.

Patterns specially prepared for workers in paper filigree were sold, and from the mid-1780s were presented with women's journals. *The New Lady's Magazine*, describing filigree work as an "art to be pursued at a very trifling expense", issued during 1786–7 a series of twelve sheets of patterns, some sixty motifs in all, designed and engraved by Styart. The competing *Lady's Magazine* for 1786 issued four plates of patterns.

Social leaders became expert workers in paper filigree. Charles Elliott, purveyor of artists' materials to the royal family, in 1791 supplied the Princess Elizabeth with "fifteen ounces of different filigree papers, one ounce of gold paper, and a box made for filigree work with ebony moulding, lock and key, lined inside and outside", also "a

79

tea caddie to correspond with the box". The craft was already declining, however, when Elinor Dashwood in Jane Austen's *Sense and Sensibility*, published 1811, offered to "roll the papers" for Lucy Steel who was occupied in making a filigree basket.

The finest filigree paper work of this period dates between the early 1780s and about 1795. *The Gentleman's Magazine* for 1791 records that an enormous number of tea-caddies with filigree paper panels were being decorated by young ladies. The well finished boxes, usually octagonal in shape, were prepared by cabinet-makers in light-coloured wood. A shallow depression in each panel and on the lid was rimmed with ivory, ebony, or, more frequently, hard-wood, sometimes elaborated with black and white stringing.

The areas within the rims were fields for filigree paper work in motifs consisting of conventional flowers, foliage and ribbons. These were made from tiny gilt-edged paper scrolls glowing superbly against a light background composed of tiny cylindrical rolls of cream or tinted paper. The interior of such a caddy was usually lined with lead paper and fitted with a loose lid also decorated with filigree paper in a design matching the outer panels.

Framed panels, known to the Georgians as picture ornaments, were usually more delicately and elaborately worked. In the majority of cases, strips of paper, folded and interlaced and twisted into peaks and spirals, were arranged as festoons or wreaths around a central panel of some other decorative medium, such as tiny wax flowers, an embroidered motif, a coloured print, a Wedgwood medallion, or a design in imitation pearls, beads and shells. The rolled-paper background was usually mounted on ivory-coloured silk measuring about 6 inches by 8 inches.

Paper filigree work also emblazoned trays, inkstands, picture-frames, fire-screens, tops of small tables, even large pieces of furniture such as cabinets. A magnificent cabinet-on-stand in the Lady Lever Art Gallery has front and sides in imitation of mosaic work surrounding coloured mezzotints after George Morland. The doors open to reveal fourteen drawers and a small cupboard each differently ornamented with paper filigree and beads.

Plate 17
Games tables. (*Top*) Mahogany with reversible top, the interior with sunk rotating chess and backgammon boards in ivory, ebony and mosaic work. From Highcliffe Castle; about 1810. (*Below*) Sofa table in satinwood, with edges cross-banded in rosewood. The reversible top slide conceals a tric-trac board; about 1800.

Plate 18
Terrestrial globes. (*Top left*) Two examples made in 1738 by John Senex, F.R.S. Diameters 12 inches and 2¾ inches. (*Top right*) On tripod stand of oak, by Dudley Adams, Fleet Street, London, 1760s. (*Lower left*) On mahogany stand, by W. and T. M. Bardin, Salisbury Square. London. About 1800. (*Lower right*) One of a pair of terrestrial and celestial globes, on mahogany stand with fluted legs. About 1800.

Few examples of paper filigree work are dated, but the period can be fixed approximately by style and methods of construction. Collectors must beware of some very poor examples produced in London early in the present century in which moulded instead of hand-made paper was used. So far no reproductions of early work have been noted.

Chapter Nine

FIRE-SCREENS: POLE AND CHEVAL

FIVE hundred years ago the Groom of the Chamber in a noble household included among his duties the provision of fuel for the chimney and a screen to protect his master from the fire whilst seated at the table (*The Boke of Curtasye, circa* 1440). The inventory of Henry VIII's domestic goods taken in 1557 shows that the king possessed "four skrynes of purple Taphata, fringed with purple silk, standying uppon feete of tymbre guilte silvered and painted". The down hearth with its cast-iron fireback reflected considerable heat into the room so that fabric screens had to be placed at some distance from the flames.

The fashion for small rooms with coal-burning grates brought into use individual fire-screens for protecting ladies from a hectic flush. The adjustable pole-screen rising from a tripod was evolved, constructed of metal. The earliest example so far recorded is included in a set of chimney furniture in the Queen's bed chamber at Ham House. This was inventoried in 1679 as a "Screen-Stick garnished with silver". It has a wrought-iron tripod with square insteps and scroll feet; vase-shaped gadrooned finials of sterling silver rising from insteps; a matching collar of silver concealing the tripod-pole joint, and a slender iron "stick" or pole terminating in an openwork finial of cast silver. The tripod and pole were originally highly burnished to match the silver. The screen panel, framed in wood, is adjustable up and down and will swing to left or right on the pole, being attached to a ring controlled by a wing screw so that it may be fixed at any desired point.

No evidence has been noted that tripod pole-screens

entirely of wood were made until the early eighteenth century. These were of walnut and their adjustable panels were arched. Mahogany was usual from the 1730s although walnut pole-screens continued to be made until the 1760s. Tripod screens followed the forms favoured for contemporaneous tripod or pillar-and-claw tables and were turned, carved and constructed by the same group of craftsmen. The slender pole rose from a sturdy turned and carved vase-shaped unit, itself supported by the tripod, each cabriole leg terminating in a carved hoof or claw foot—occasionally a paw. The knees might be smooth or carved, often with a shell motif. In the early walnut examples the spread of the tripod was less expansive and the vase motif shorter than in fine mahogany tripods. The slender rod was finished with a small finial, usually in vase or pineapple shape.

The screen panel was surrounded by a flat-surfaced frame, with square-cut edge such as was painted by Hogarth in Scene II, "Mariage à la Mode", 1744. The main purpose of this frame was to act as a stretcher for the ornamental needlework it displayed.

Chippendale illustrates fashionable fire-screens with poles in his *Director*, 1754, describing them as "pillars and claws among the best of their sort". These display a wealth of rococo C-curves and ornate design typical of the Louis XV style. The concave, boldly carved tripod, with either upward or downward scrolling feet, supports an open-work three-sided pedestal and from its top rises the vertical pole terminating in an expansive carved finial such as a vase of flowers or a pagoda hung with silver bells. Such screens measured about five feet in height, tripod and openwork pedestal each measuring about a foot.

The frame enclosing the needlework panel might be very narrow, its front surface semi-circular in section, or moulded or carved with repeating motifs. Alternatively it was wider with carved decoration at each rounded corner, or resembled the wide frames, carved with scrollwork and flowers, used for framing oil paintings. Chippendale recommended that screen frames should measure 16 inches wide and 18½ inches deep, but existing examples show that widths ranging from 20 to 27 inches were preferred for screening the heat. The majority were plainly rectangular: some had arched tops which might have low openwork crestings.

Pole-screens were now fashionably made in pairs, one for each side of the fireplace. The embroidered panels seldom matched but were designed to harmonise. In 1758 Dr. Johnson was interested to note that "we have twice as many fire-screens as chimneys". This was not invariably so, however, for in 1765 the cabinet-maker William Vile of St. Martin's Lane invoiced George III, "For the Queen's use a neat mahogany pillar and claw screen, neatly carv'd, to her Majesty's piece of Needlework, £3.10s.".

Pole-screens with openwork pedestals and rococo tripods are shown on three trade cards illustrating Sir Ambrose Heal's *London Furniture Makers* (1953). Two of these issued during the 1770s were designed and engraved by Mathias Darly who engraved many of Chippendale's designs. Thomas Porter, New Round Court, shows a tripod constructed entirely of scroll units, a triangular shelf separating two superimposed tripods supporting the pole. Lander, of No. 48 Chandos Street, illustrates a pole-screen with a tall openwork tripod carved in rococo scrollwork. Tripod and pole are of equal length and topped by a Chinese pagoda ornament. The narrow rimmed frame has clipped corners. Pillars of engaged columns date from about 1760, the cabriole leg is now replaced by the scroll leg.

The pole-screen frame usually enclosed a panel of embroidery worked by one of the ladies of the house, and given the advantage of conspicuous display. A young lady of fashion, according to *Ladies Conduct*, 1722, "cannot amuse herself more genteely than by learning the art of drawing, as this will be a considerable advantage to her if she has any inclination to fine curious work such as embroidery for chairs and screens". For many screen panels tent stitch was used on fine canvas. Alternatively, only the figures or floral motifs were in fine tent stitch with a background of cross stitch. Wool, silk, and silver-gilt or silver threads might be used for the embroidery.

The motif of grouped flowers in a vase or basket was in favour: but pastoral scenes, Biblical subjects, groups showing a lady and her gallant, were more frequent. For floral

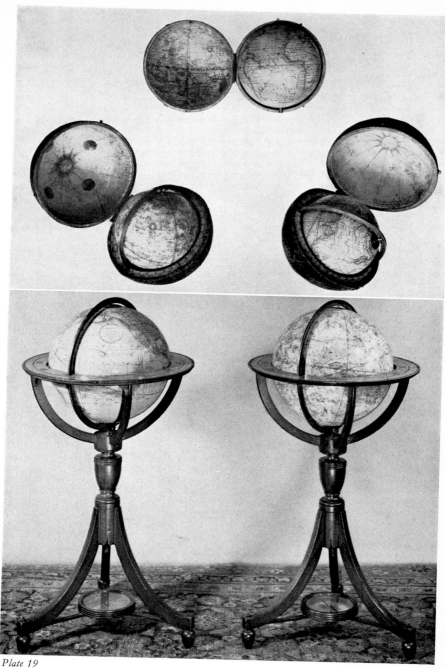

Plate 19
Terrestrial globes. (*Top*) Three pocket globes by Newton Brothers, 97 Chancery Lane, London. Late eighteenth century. (*Lower*) Pair of globes, terrestrial and celestial, on mahogany stands, each with a compass below. Height 35 inches. Dated 1800.

Plate 20
(*Top*) A pair of japanned knife and fork boxes enriched with gilded ornament; complete with 12 silver-handled knives and forks. Late seventeenth century. (*Bottom*) A pair of knife, fork and spoon boxes in yew wood and marquetry work, with silver mounts and handles. About 1770.

designs the needlewoman might have recourse to Furber's *Four Hundred Curious Representations of the most Beautiful Flowers*, 1734, or Heckell's *Select Collection of the most Beautiful Flowers drawn after Nature and Disposed in their Proper Order in Baskets*, undated. The colour value of these panels was always highly appreciated. Needlework designs for pole-screen panels might be copied from mezzotint reproductions of oil paintings: sometimes on a silk panel the flesh tints were in water colours. Coats of arms, amorini and classical landscapes have been noted.

From the 1760s, comparatively few panels were worked in *petit point* and slighter, less laborious forms of embroidery were more popular. Horace Walpole refers to pole-screens "worked in chenille, to suit with the chimney, by the Countess of Ailesbury". Painted and gilded leather was used, too, red and green moroccos being favourites, often in the same design as the painted leather on chairs. The back of a screen frame was usually covered with decorative material. One inventory records that "ye back is Lyned with India paper", and papered backs have been noted painted with oriental scenes.

The classical mood advocated by Robert Adam reduced pole-screens to smaller dimensions. The framed panels now merely screened the face and their lighter weight made them easier to adjust. Such pole-screens are frequent domestic accessories illustrated in paintings and prints of the late eighteenth century. Johann Zoffany's conversation piece "The Dutton Family" shows a fashionable drawing-room of about 1780. Beside the fireplace is a pole-screen with a small vertical rectangular panel of flower embroidery screening the face of Mrs Dutton.

The woods displayed were now mahogany, satinwood and rosewood, although from the 1770s japanned and painted beech was used more frequently, often in colours matching japanned and painted furniture in the same room. Carved and gilded pole-screens also belong to this period. Legs tended to sprawl and in place of the cabriole legs the 1780s saw many concave curves. The legs extended from a heavy urn-shaped unit with a turned, pointed finial below. Hepplewhite in 1788 illustrated a new type consisting of a

85

solid shaft rising from a turned circular foot weighted with lead or an asphalt-pumice mixture to ensure stability. The foot usually stood directly on the floor, but might be supported by a plinth or a stumpy claw-and-ball tripod.

Large rectangular panels were succeeded by ovals, shield-shapes, circles and squares usually veneered, as well as various indented outlines associated with the new formalised "fan" motifs of the period. By the 1780s shields and ovals were made to match those of the chair backs in the same room, but the rectangular form continued to be used as well.

Hepplewhite states in his *Guide*, 1788, that pole-screens "may be ornamented variously with maps, Chinese figures, needlework, etc.". Silk embroidery upon a silk or satin ground was fashionable, and there was a minor fashion for black and white imitations of line engravings in extremely minute stitches of silk or hair. Filigree paper work panels were used during the 1780s and 1790s (see Chapter 8). To protect such a panel from dust it was glazed, the frame being rabbeted to hold the glass, with similar shaping at the back fitted with a straining board to prevent the frame from warping and cracking the glass. Decoration might be painted upon the straining board. Gathered silk was a favoured style of pole-screen backing at this time, also protected with glazing.

Thomas Sheraton for his *Drawing Book*, 1791-1793, devised a number of pole-screens supported on particularly slender claw legs in concave or convex curves and raised on long, square, tapering feet. Creating a demand for so-called patent furniture, he made fashionable pole-screens in which the pole, square in section, was drilled vertically with a round hole, and a pulley-and-cord mechanism fitted into an urn-shaped unit beneath the pole. A weight was concealed in the cord-tassel hanging below. The screen could be balanced at any desired height merely by a touch. A strengthening member consisted of a brass ring, with a scalloped lower rim, gilded and burnished, joining the legs at their deepest curves. Sheraton recommends such screens to be made of mahogany or to be japanned or in white and gold.

Pole-screens with the oval and heart-shaped panels now generally referred to as the Hepplewhite style continued to be made in large numbers, often with tall, spindly tripods inlaid with lines in a contrasting wood and fitted with reeded lion paw feet. The firm of Allen, on a trade card issued in about 1800, illustrates a shield-shaped frame with a highly domed crest.

In the early nineteenth century pole-screens became more colourful and ornamental, designs being adapted from French Empire styles. Demand was greater than in the eighteenth century. The solid base or block continued popular and might now be triangular with a scroll foot at each corner, the upper surface enriched with gilded brass ornament. The pole might rise directly from such a base, thicker than formerly and turned in a single piece with a solid fluted pedestal.

The legs in the tripod design were short and plain, the pillar approximating double their height: the majority were built from units. A pole-screen with a short tripod tended to be enriched with gilded brass and a large, heavy finial and a spun brass domed collar concealing the pedestal-pole joint; the lower legs might be reeded and mounted on lion paw feet. Carving was sometimes gilded. In many examples a flat triangular shelf was fixed immediately above the tripod paws and although intended for strengthening purposes this could serve as a foot-rest if desired. Rosewood was most frequently used during the Regency years, but inlaid and painted satinwood, carved and gilded lime wood, amboyna, mahogany and pine are found.

Thomas Hope in *Household Furniture and Interior Decoration*, 1807, illustrates pole-screens intended for his home at Deepdene, Surrey. These are of rosewood with carved and gilded enrichments, the design consisting of a brass pole with a lance-shaped finial bearing a shield of rosewood carved with a classical thunderbolt.

The vogue for pole-screens displaying oil paintings started a few years later. The pictures were painted on copper plates or sheets of papier-mâché, and their gilded frames might be square, hexagonal or octagonal. These were succeeded by pole-screens of papier-mâché throughout, pole and expansive pedestal foot being enriched with gilding.

SMALL ANTIQUE FURNITURE

Banner pole-screens date from about 1813 and were advertised until mid-Victorian days. In these a piece of textile, such as damask or velvet fringed with tassels, was suspended, unframed, from a carved cross-bar adjustable on the pole. Pole-screens displaying embroidery continued until mid-Victorian times. As late as 1870 Mrs. Oliphant noted in her *Diary*: "I have just finished the most enchanting pole screen."

Cheval fire-screens joined pole-screens at the English fireside in the 1690s with other newly acquired house furnishings from Holland, and became known as horse fire-screens. Bailey's dictionary, 1730, defines "horse" as "a Piece of Wood jointed across two other perpendicular ones". The Frenchified name cheval fire-screen appears to have been of Regency origin so far as England is concerned, coming into use after the close of the Napoleonic wars in 1815. The first reference so far noted is in *Ackermann's Repository*, 1818.

At first these fire-screens were constructed from soft, easily worked woods such as well-seasoned beech, ornately carved, gilded and burnished. A pair of sturdy uprights rising from heavy scrolled trestle feet were connected by a deep stretcher and contained a rectangular straight-topped panel with a high ornamental curved and pierced cresting. The panel might be a fixture, but more frequently was designed to slide up and down against the flat backs of the uprights, held in any desired position by two flat springs. This adjustable panel contained either a needlework picture, a piece of tapestry or heavy red velvet.

These lavishly carved and gilded screens were costly but continued fashionable accessories with other gilt furniture in the great houses of the restoration period. Chippendale illustrates three examples in the 1762 edition of his *Director* describing them as "standing on four Feet, and commonly called Horse-Fire-Screens: the Wood-work of all of them should be gilt in burnished Gold". This plate, No. CLVIII, was engraved by W. Foster in 1761, so that these designs must have been in height of current fashion and not merely perpetuated from the 1754 edition of the *Director*. The frames are of irregular cartouche outline, floridly carved and pierced. Two of them have fixed panels: Chippendale notes

88

of the third that "the panel is intended to slide up, out of the pillars that are on each side". He provides, too, a marginal sketch showing the construction of the pillar-stretcher-foot joint. The pillar or upright at each end is set into a narrow block and the feet are tenoned into the ends of this, while the stretcher is tenoned into the inner side.

For lesser homes from early in the eighteenth century cabinet-makers designed cheval screens of lighter pattern, usually in walnut. Japanned cheval screens, it appears, were not made until late in the century as the great heat thrown out from the open grates caused them to blister and flake. Their uprights were turned, their trestle feet scrolled and the high cresting carved in elaborate openwork, occasionally centred with the owner's crest as on many a gilded screen. The stretcher might be turned, moulded or carved in a style to harmonise with the cresting. The top of the panel remained straight until about 1715 when it was made slightly arched with rounded corners, but still retaining its openwork cresting. By 1740 the cresting was solid with carved edging and a central motif such as an escallop shell or a medallion. The uprights might be turned in columnar form and sunk with grooves in which the sliding panel would move smoothly up and down. By 1740 the trestle at each end of the screen had been replaced by a triangular block fitted with short cabriole legs carved on the knees and on the club or claw-and-ball feet.

Fashionable eighteenth-century panels might be filled on both sides of the frame with water-colour paintings in Chinese style on Indian paper. One of these might be replaced eventually by a *petit point* panel worked by one of the family. Less frequently coloured maps or oil paintings were used. In 1732 Benjamin Goodison, a well-known cabinet-maker of The Golden Spread Eagle, Long Acre, made to the order of the Princess Royal "two walnut tree fire screens with sliding frames covered with Indian paper on both sides". The size of a cheval fire-screen until the 1740s approximated 4 feet 6 inches in height with a width of about 3 feet.

Mahogany then became the fashionable wood, more costly than walnut and harder to work. The size of cheval

89

screens consequently was reduced to an average height of 3 feet 6 inches and a width of 2 feet. Instead of turned pillars and stretchers, square-cut units were used, their flat surfaces being sunk and carved with geometrical and wave designs associated with the period's chairs, back and front carved to match. Stretchers were generally pierced and might have fretted brackets in the lower corners.

The cresting of these mahogany screens was shallower and less ornate than formerly. Frequently it introduced symmetrically arranged acanthus scrolls carved and pierced, or acanthus foliage flanking an escallop shell and suspending husk festoons down the uprights. Scrolled legs might be carved on the knees with shells and husk pendants, and have scrolled toes.

A cheval screen of the 1760s and 1770s might have a top in serpentine outline surmounted by two ivory vase-shaped finials, the curved legs terminating in block toes. Formerly, panel and leg proportions had been about equal: legs now became higher, the panel shorter.

Two-leaf folding fire-screens competed with cheval and pole-screens between the early 1740s and the 1770s. Each leaf consisted of a square panel supported upon two slender legs, sometimes connected with a stretcher, the two leaves being hinged centrally. Such screens, measuring about 3 feet 6 inches in height and each leaf 20 inches wide, were easily lifted. But they were fragile and few are known to remain. Horace Walpole in his description of Strawberry Hill refers to a two-leaf fire-screen containing part of a map of Surrey and Middlesex which he notes "is a piece of the first tapestry woven in England".

Chippendale in the first edition of his *Director*, 1754, illustrates three examples engraved from his drawings by Mathias Darly, a well-known designer of furniture. Two are panelled in the Chinese fretted style supported by legs and stretchers in carved rococo style. The third example is fully rococo. Each panel is fitted with a Chinese painting on paper, Chippendale mentioning that "the Fret which goes round the India Paper is cut through". There might be Chinese paintings in colours back and front of each panel. Mezzotints, water colours and painting on silk have been recorded also, set in folding fire-screens. From about 1760 there was a cresting above each panel and an apron below.

Hepplewhite in his *Guide*, 1788, continues the term "Horse-Fire-Screen" and recommends them to be made in mahogany or japanned wood. The cheval fire-screen now stood on four boldly convex claw legs, sometimes moulded on the upper surface and terminating in scroll feet. These were taller than the former legs and lifted the panel clear of the user's feet while still protecting her face. There might now be two stretchers, one above the other, square or rectangular in section and tenoned directly into the uprights which usually terminated in gilded or ivory vase finials.

The panel, which might be sliding or fixed, contained an oval centre-piece, the former pictorial devices still being usual although now there was the alternative of gathered silk. Apparently the main weakness in the screen's design was the condition of the springs which held the sliding panel in the grooves of the upright and made it adjustable. Frequent replacements were required. Hepplewhite overcame this by fitting hand-screws which held the panel firmly in any desired position. The screws might operate at the sides or the back, but the device was never widely used, possibly because of the introduction of stronger spring steel in the 1790s.

Sheraton writing in *The Cabinet Dictionary*, 1803, comments that horse-fire-screens with sliding panels were common and that those framing fine prints should be protected with glass. Legs were higher and their convex curve bolder than formerly. The recommended height was 3 feet 6 inches and breadth 18 inches. A stretcher was inserted to link the uprights, which were enriched with sheaths of gilded brass ornament, frequently based on acanthus foliage motifs. Sheraton illustrates several patterns, one with a shield-shaped panel and a cresting of carved flowers and other motifs. He also advocates the three-panel screen, the centre a fixture with panels to slide left and right. This required extensive trestle feet to ensure stability. Loudon's *Encyclopaedia*, 1833, illustrates a fire-screen with a central leaf sliding upward and two leaves hinging left and right.

Cheval screens in rosewood, walnut and maple appeared in the 1840s set with panels of thick, wide bevelled plate glass. But soon there were other alternatives. At the Great Exhibition, 1851, Thomas Nicoll, a well-known London furniture manufacturer, showed "a Cheval Screen, carved in soft wood and gilt: it is so constructed that by withdrawing four bolts it may be converted into a stand for lights, a music stand and a chess or coffee table. The panel frames a Pastil Painting on vellum". The frame was a complicated design of scrollwork and flowers with a central motif in the cresting containing an urn with a pair of amorini. Similar screens were advertised by other makers as "multiformia". At the same time there was a vogue for cheval screens in walnut closely resembling early Georgian specimens with solid and pierced crestings and with the frames enclosing brilliantly coloured machine-made tapestries or flower groups in Berlin woolwork.

There was a great Victorian demand for papier-mâché trestle cheval fire-screens. On an ornate example the frame was a mass of openwork, dust-catching enrichments and there might be an infant Bacchus set upon each trestle foot. The frame bore a papier-mâché panel painted with a scene, such as one of the Oxford colleges—there were about a hundred pictures in the series painted by Spiers of Oxford—a cathedral interior, or a copy of a celebrated painting. Less elaborate framing might surround one of Lane's patent pearl glass pictures, with laminated mother-of-pearl fixed behind glass on which the picture was painted.

Writing fire-screens for ladies were designed in the 1780s and continued in production until the 1850s. The *Cabinet-Maker's London Book of Prices*, 1788, illustrates such a screen built on the lines of a cheval screen with an open space below. The panel became a vertical box-like container for pigeon-holes and shelves or needlework fitments with a falling flap for reading or work. George Smith illustrates a "cheval screen libraire" in his *Cabinet Maker's and Upholsterer's Guide*, 1826, in which the uprights support bookshelves concealed behind a screen of pleated silk.

Plate 21

(*Left*) A pair of urn-shaped knife and fork cases in satinwood enriched with stringing between the panels and at the corners. (*Centre*) Urn-shaped knife, fork and spoon case in satinwood with painted decoration; about 1780. (*Right*) One of a pair of urns on pedestals, one urn lined with lead to hold water. Made by John Linnell in 1767.

Plate 22

Wall lanterns. (*Top left*) Mahogany enriched with monsters' heads and acanthus motifs in ormolu. (*Top right*) Mahogany with mirror back and carved frame and with the sides hinged to open. (*Lower left*) Walnut with mirror back and base and the front hinging in a single piece. The brass hook is for hanging a glass smoke shade. (*Lower right*) One of a pair of wall lanterns in mahogany carved and gilded. From Norfolk House, St. James's Square.

Chapter Ten

GAMES TABLES

BACKGAMMON was a favourite game in the English home a thousand years ago when indoor amusements were few. The game was played on a square board, painted or incised to mark the twenty-four points. Illuminated manuscripts of the twelfth century show players with such a board, the pieces being moved in accordance with the throw of a dice.

The game was then known as tables, the board as a table, the player as a tabler, and the pieces as tablemen, at a period when the table in its modern sense was termed a board. The name backgammon does not appear to have been used earlier than the reign of Charles I. There is doubt regarding its origin, but a plausible explanation is that it was derived from a combination of the Welsh *bach*—little—and *cammaun*—battle. When in the fourteenth century the reverse of the board was marked for newly introduced draughts, then known as chequers, the complete board was termed a pair of tables, each surface being counted as a separate table. The name chequers was given to many an ale-house and inn where such a board was at the disposal of customers. A pair of tables in common wood at this time cost fourpence; in 1583 the price was eightpence.

In 1519 Horman recorded that he had "bought a playing tabull, with XII poyntes on the one side and chekers on the other side". Luxury sets might be made of hard wood set with mother-of-pearl and ebony, the men turned from ivory and ebony. A pair of tables might be accompanied by a three-legged table upon which it rested during play. This, variously spelt, was described as "a paire of Tabyls tabelle".

Women, it appeared, were not encouraged to play at tables. In 1540 Hyrde exclaimed "What a foule thing it is, to see a woman in steade of her woolbasket, to handle the tablebourd". Nevertheless, inventories taken during the sixteenth century demonstrate that most well-established families possessed at least one pair of tables. That at Marketon, Derbyshire, was described in 1545 as "a square payr of tables with the men of boxe red and white xij^d". The Earl of Northampton's inventory of 1614 included "a paire of tables of Ebony inlaied with Ivorie and men suteable xx[•]". In addition there was "one cabinett of purple velvett with chesse boord and men suteable laced with gold lace x^{li}".

The pair of tables made in a piece with a "tables' table" appears to date no earlier than the reign of Elizabeth I. In this design the double top folded in the same way as a Georgian card table. The upper leaf opened back on to a pair of horizontal pull-out supports, the exposed interior being inlaid to form a table for backgammon and draughts. An example in oak is preserved at Penshurst Place, Kent.

The reign of Charles II was marked by the development in London of much colourful, elegant furniture. This included walnut card tables which, when not in use, had their superbly grained surfaces covered with cloths of green silken velvet embroidered and fringed with gold thread. The card table and backgammon, chess and draught boards were soon combined into a single piece of handsome furniture.

The new games table, now extremely rare, was of walnut with three rectangular leaves. The top leaf was lifted over to rest on one of the back legs which swung out to support it. The centre of the square card table thus formed was covered with green silk velvet glued in position, its edges concealed beneath braid lightly woven from gold thread. In addition the velvet might be encircled with a single row of gilt-headed nails. The second flap lifted to form a table-top veneered with burr or oyster walnut inset with holly, lignum vitae or other distinctive woods forming the squares and triangular points required for chess, draughts and backgammon. The third leaf when lifted disclosed a receptacle for storing players' materials—cards, chessmen, draughts, dice, counters and so on. This could be locked.

The open leaves were supported at first by the gate-table method. The whole of one of the back legs, attached to an arm hinged to the back framing, swung out to support the leaf at a predetermined position. Sometimes two legs were movable, and sometimes a fifth leg served this purpose. A more convenient but elaborate method came into use during the reign of George I. The back of the underframing, complete with the two back legs, could be drawn out on a triple-hinged concertina device. The result was a square underframe with a leg at each corner. When the table was closed the extension folded on to itself.

The edges of walnut tables were rounded and had projecting corners shaped as segments of a circle, which, when the flaps were opened, revealed circular slightly sunk receptacles for candlestick bases. Four oval receptacles were sunk into the table top for the players' coins or counters. Legs were cabriole or straight with bun feet and at first were uncarved.

Games tables in mahogany began to be introduced from about 1730, and the mood lent itself to splendidly bold carving in the fiercely naturalistic style of George II's day. Masks and shell motifs carved on the knees might be enhanced by open-scroll or other enrichment on the shoulders. Feet were then of the ball-and-claw design. Corner projections might now be square and fitted with pull-out trays, inlaid or silk-lined, for supporting candlesticks in the more angular, square-based early Georgian designs. A drawer customarily replaced the locker in the underframing and occupied the same position. The two brass handles were matched by a keyhole escutcheon between them. From the 1720s the feet of such tables were often mounted on castors with broad leather rollers. It was usual to arrange the tables against the wall when not in use and the castors facilitated their removal to the playing position by fireside or window.

The great gambling era quickened people's wits and from the mid-eighteenth century came a revival of a complicated form of backgammon known as tric-trac, so-called from the clicking sound made by the pieces during play. As early as 1687 Sedly, in *Bellamira*, differentiated between backgammon and tric-trac: "I lost three sets at backgammon and about at tric-trac." *The Gentleman's Magazine* of 1788 refers to several different kinds of tric-trac. The backgammon board intended also for tric-trac is distinguished by a shallow gallery surrounding the flat playing area, a feature found in most games tables from the late 1760s, and in a few examples dating from the 1740s.

The mahogany games table was adapted to accommodate a tric-trac board, sunken and divided into two parts. Such a table at first was made square with a wide carved or moulded underframe, the top containing a movable panel secured by a pair of trigger catches designed to appear as drawer knobs. When pulled they permitted the panel to be lifted from its frame. The upper surface of the panel was veneered; on the reverse it was inlaid with contrasting woods for use as a draughts board, with a small ivory rectangle inset on either side pierced for pegging the score at cribbage.

Removal of the panel revealed a shallow recess in which tric-trac was played on a mahogany board with points of contrasting colour which might be either inlaid, painted, or tooled on leather. The front of this tric-trac recess was fitted with a pair of dummy drawer handles in brass. Beneath the recess was a deepish drawer extending the full width of the table and fitted with handles matching those above. A pair of pull-out candlestick slides fitted beneath two sides of such a table. Some of these games tables have plain square legs chambered on the inner angle, or a simple cabriole form with the popular cyma curve outlining the apron.

The trigger mechanism was abandoned by about 1770 in favour of a central leaf running the full width of the new rectangular table top and sliding into position on tongues and grooves. The joints between the sliding leaf and table top could only be seen by close inspection. Games tables of this type were ingeniously secreted in tables outwardly intended for other purposes, such as sofa tables. Table and slide were veneered and polished as a single entity and might be bordered with inlaid lines of holly, lignum vitae or box. The beautifully figured mahogany of the period produced some lovely colour shadings in the best work.

Gamesters, requiring tables to seat only two players,

Plate 23

Hall lanterns. (*Top left*) In iron with applied ormolu enrichment in the Adam style. (*Top right*) Square portable wall lantern with mirror back and base, and its brass frame set with painted enamel ornament. (*Lower left and right*) Two hall lanterns in designs illustrated by Thomas Chippendale in plate CLIII of *The Gentleman and Cabinet Maker's Director*, 1762 edition. The lantern on the left, in mahogany carved and gilded, and about 8 feet high, was formerly at St Dunstan's House, Regent's Park and is now in the Metropolitan Museum, New York. That on the right is in a six-panelled pear shape.

7+

Plate 24
Papier-mâché furniture. (*Top left*) A paper-ware teapoy decorated with conventional flowers and peacocks, the latter a subject associated with Frederick Newman who worked for the firm of Shoolbred, Loveridge and Shoolbred, Wolverhampton. (*Top right*) Teapoy of pulped papier-mâché japanned black and painted with flower motifs in full colour with gilded scroll-work. (*Lower left*) Chair with a musical seat playing three tunes. The back panel is decorated with a flower spray in nautilus shell. (*Lower right*) Chair in black japanned pressed papier-mâché. The back panel is painted with Warwick Castle in oils, the openwork surround ornamented with shell and bronze work.

apparently preferred rectangular trestle-end tables to the square or circular four-legged tables required by card players. The end supports, reinforced by a strong central stretcher, adequately withstood the strain of movement when the table was wheeled to playing position on the brass castors which, by the 1770s, had superseded the leather-wheeled type. The wide spread of the trestle feet beneath the narrow ends of the table top prevented the table from tilting if an onlooker happened to lean on one of the short leaves hinged at the ends of the playing section. These were supported by fly brackets hinged to the underframing, replacing the candlestick slides. In some tables of this type the ends had a pierced metal gallery, usually of gilded brass alloy, intended to prevent candlesticks, decanters and drinking glasses from accidentally slipping to the floor.

Decoration on the tops of late eighteenth-century games tables followed the style of other furniture whether in inlay, marquetry or paint. This consisted of a conventional border surrounding a central panel of finely figured veneer in mahogany, walnut, tiger wood, calamander wood, satinwood, or other decorative wood, often edged with ebony stringing, sometimes set with a stylised fan or flower shape.

Makers of the fine, intricate marquetry known as Tunbridge ware gave much of their attention to the requirements of various games, and produced some highly ornate games tables. Indeed their popular vandyke patterns which preceded and sometimes accompanied the early nineteenth-century mosaic work may have been inspired by the backgammon points.

Games tables outwardly resembling square urn tables with cross-stretchers joining the legs were made during the 1780s and 1790s. The top comprised a reversible panel, the lower side inlaid with squares for playing chess and draughts, covering a partitioned tric-trac and backgammon board. The front of this shallow well was designed as a sham drawer with a real drawer below fitted with lock and two handles. Two hinged leaves might hang down the sides, supported by folding brackets when in use, or there might be a pair of pull-out candlestick slides. The cross-stretchers, of square

7*

THERLE HUGHES

Fig. 3.   Games Tables

section when accompanying square legs and turned when with turned legs, braced the legs a few inches above floor level. Similar games tables were later supported on sturdy pedestals, usually a solid plinth from four outward curved legs with brass lion-paw feet.

Rosewood games tables date from about 1800. These introduced a new fashion: the table top was constructed as a hollow, three-compartment box, rather squarer than a true ellipse. The curved ends were fitted with hinged lids, forming a pair of D-shaped wells for the reception of games materials. A tongued-and-grooved central sliding panel covered a tric-trac board. In some examples the shaped ends were merely flaps as in earlier designs supported by hinged fly brackets. Such a games table was supported on a pair of horse legs, each consisting of two turned uprights rising from a pair of outspreading feet, usually with concave curves and fitted with brass castors. Three turned stretchers joined each pair of legs.

The demand for games tables during the last decade of the eighteenth century prompted Georgian cabinet-makers to combine in a single piece of furniture a games table, dressing table and desk. Others were provided with treble tops so that a single piece served as a card table, chess board, backgammon board, reading lectern and writing desk. So cleverly were joints disguised between the various sliding panels that some of these tables may not yet have revealed all their secrets.

Sewing or pouch tables with silk covered bags for the work in hand and drawers to contain sewing accessories were made in such a way that they could be transformed quickly into games tables. Sheraton illustrates such tables in his *Cabinet Maker and Upholsterer's Drawing Book* (1791–1793). One type of combination work-and-games table was

---

GAMES TABLES

1. Early eighteenth century with three folding leaves—for chess and backgammon (as shown), for cards and for writing. There are drawers for playing and writing materials. 2. Piquet table of about 1700. 3. Mid-eighteenth-century table with two folding leaves. 4. The lift-off chess board reveals a tric-trac recess. There is also a top of finely figured wood to make this an occasional table. 5 and 5a. Bagatelle table, late eighteenth century. The closed top is marked for chess and backgammon. Sham drawers at the end. 6. Pembroke table with sliding chessboard (reversible) over tric-trac recess. 7. End-of-century games table reduced to the minimum required for chess and tric-trac and for candles to illuminate the play. 8. Regency design with brass inlay and ormolu mounts. The leather-lined top lifts for reading and under it is a tric-trac well. Drawers at the sides hold the games materials. 9. Sofa table with tric-trac recess under the sliding reversible chess board. The drawers are sham. 10. Brass inlaid rosewood Regency games table with hinged ends covering recesses for the playing materials.

made with a double-hinged top similar to the larger card tables. A shallow pull-out drawer was for backgammon: a second and deeper drawer below contained scissors, spools, and other needlework equipment, with a deep bag-like receptacle sliding in and out beneath the table frame. More attractively this receptacle might be constructed of decorative veneered wood, for the folds of the silk tended to collect dust and became rusty-looking.

Ackermann's Repository, 1811, illustrates a design for a table "comprehending seven different accommodations". At first glance the piece appears to be a reading or writing table, but by sliding the desk off a games table is revealed. Underneath is a silk pouch for needlework. This table was made by the firm of Morgan and Sanders. Several designs for combination pieces are illustrated in George Smith's *Household Furniture*, 1808, and he wrote that the interior must be "covered entirely with leather to prevent noise when used in play". The projecting ends—a feature of Smith's games tables—contained concealed drawers to hold the chess and backgammon pieces. In some instances the upper surface was inlaid as a chessboard, in others the chessboard drew out while the top was fitted with a rising desk supported on a ratchet.

Chapter Eleven

GLOBES

"A DESCRIPTION of the world on a solid sphere . . ." as early as 1497 the Duke of Milan received a despatch from London thus prefectly defining a terrestrial globe and describing one made by the great John Cabot (1450–1498) whose voyages were the boast of Bristol. This probably was the earliest English specimen of these fascinating, evocative tributes to men's determination to comprehend the world. But already on the continent a major advance in the making of globes had been accomplished. Until 1492 the globe had been entirely of metal, usually gilded brass, but with silver, silver-gilt, copper and copper-gilt as possible alternatives. Upon this the map had to be engraved. Then Martin Behaim founded a new craft in Nuremburg, constructing simple globes by pasting layer upon layer of linen over a mould, covering it with parchment and drawing a map upon its surface. The sphere revolved within a metal meridian and a metal horizon circle supported upon a tripod stand. Early in the sixteenth century globes were built from papier-mâché composition shaped over a mould and covered with a thick layer of plaster and finished with strips of paper or parchment upon which the map was drawn by hand.

The great advance, dating to about 1510, was the introduction of printing, from copper plates or wood blocks. This necessitated the use of paper cut into a number of shaped gores that could be printed flat then fastened exactly over the globe's surface. This required careful adjustment and manipulation, and rules were evolved for globe-gore construction which remain unaltered today.

Globes manufactured in the Netherlands by Gerhard

Mercator were used in England until the 1590s. A damaged example shows them to have been constructed from thin, narrow strips of wood covered with cloth followed by a thin layer of plaster. Over this again was applied a composition of plaster, sawdust and glue, about ¼-inch thick. Upon this prepared surface were pasted the printed gores. Mercator truncated his gores twenty degrees from each pole, covering the remaining polar spaces with a pair of circular printed discs.

England's first professional globe-maker was Emery Molyneux of whom Hakluyt in the preface to his *Principall Navigations*, observed: "I have contented myselfe with inserting one of the best general mappes of the world onely, untill the coming out of a very large and most exact terrestrial globe, collected and reformed according to the newest, secretest, and latest discoveries, both Spanish, Portugal and English, composed by M. Emmerie Mollineux of Lambeth, a rare, gentleman in his profession, being therein for divers yeeres greatly supported by the purse and liberalitie of the worshipful merchant, Mr. William Sanderson."

A manual on Molyneux globes, published in 1592 by Robert Hues, describes their stands: "First of all there is a base, on which there is raised perpendicularly six Columnes or Pillars of equal length and distance, upon the top of which there is fastened a levell parallel to the Base, a round plate or circle of wood, and a sufficient breadth and thickness which they call the Horizon. Upon this is painted the zodiac signs, months, roman calendar, points of the compass in concentric circles." Into this stand was fitted the globe which had a hollow wooden sphere as its basis. This was a purely English feature that established a reputation for long life and accuracy, and prompted a considerable export trade throughout the seventeenth and eighteenth centuries.

Such a terrestrial globe, with a matching celestial globe, stood in the long gallery at Northampton House, Greenwich. In the inventory taken after the Earl of Northampton's death in 1614 they were described as "a paire of Molineux globes covered with green taffata" and valued at four pounds. Such a pair of Molyneux globes, 26 inches in diameter, is preserved in the library of Middle Temple.

Little is known of the individual globe-makers until after the mid-seventeenth century when several London map-makers engaged in the work. The core of an English globe was a sphere of soft wood, rather less in size that the finished globe. Into the poles were driven two metal rods. This unit was known as the axis and formed the basis of the entire structure. A hollow globe was then made from paper, glued layer after layer over a spherical mould to a depth of $\frac{1}{16}$ inch. When dry and hard this was cut around the circumference with a sharp knife. The pair of hemispherical caps thus formed were slipped from the mould, placed over the rods of the axis and their edges sewn together with pack thread.

The globe had now to be provided with a smooth, hard outer surface. It was fitted into an iron semi-circle of the size intended for the finished globe and a composition of whiting, glue and water melted together and thickly smeared over the paper surface. As the plaster was applied the axis was revolved in the semi-circle, the edge of which pared off superfluous composition. When dry the ball was returned to the semi-circle and a fresh coating of composition applied. This process of alternately applying composition and drying it was continued until the ball was of the correct size with a perfectly smooth surface ready to receive the map.

The map was printed in heavy black outline from copper plates. There were twelve, eighteen or thirty-six gores covering thirty, twenty or ten degrees longitude and extending through the equator to about the 67th parallels north and south. When mounted upon the globe together with the polar discs, a complete map was formed, the lines of longitude helping to conceal the almost invisible joints. Before attachment to the globe, the mounter, with the aid of a semi-circle, drew guide lines upon its surface, out-lining the appropriate number of gores. When moistened with adhesive the paper gores expanded, thus increasing the difficulty of perfect co-ordination and the avoidance of slight folds. Expansion differed with various papers making it essential for a test to be carried out beforehand. The possibility of the gores shrinking whilst drying was over-come by the presence of glue in the surface composition.

North and south poles were then pasted in position. An

improvement was made in the preparation of polar discs from about 1700. A very narrow segment was cut from each disc decreasing the angle from 360 degrees to 350: when damp the paper stretched to cover the required 360 degrees.

The map was then coloured by an illuminator using transparent water colours, applied sparingly so that printed outlines and names were clearly visible. The colours used until the end of the eighteenth century were red (red ink); blue (litmus); green (sap green and verdigris in vinegar); yellow (gamboge, yellow berry or turmeric); purple (log wood); brown (Spanish liquorice); black (Indian ink). Adjoining colours were, of course, in contrasting hues. When dry the map was varnished for protection and to resist damp and prevent dust from being rubbed into the paper.

The globe was hung in a brass meridian with an hour circle, and a quadrant of altitude, and then fitted into the horizon circle of a wooden stand. To prevent the colours from bleaching in sunlight, globes were covered with green baize: the later globes in cabinet-made mahogany stands were covered with green or red morocco leather.

Map-makers printed stock sets of gores in several sizes for sale to the globe-makers, with blank cartouches for overprinting the globe-maker's name and a description of the map. Many copper plates were in use for as long as a century, their original dates unaltered although sometimes up-to-date information was added. Such globes are found fitted into stands of a much later period than their printed dates suggest. A list of standard sizes with prices was issued in 1683 by Joseph Moxon, Sign of the Atlas, Ludgate Hill. The globes were sold in pairs, the terrestrial globe being accompanied by the celestial, defined by Bailey in his dictionary, 1730, as one "Upon whose Superficies is painted the Images of the Constellations and the fixed Stars, with the Circles of the Spheres". The prices, with matching stands, were: 26 inches diameter, £20; 15 inches £4; 8 inches £2; and 6 inches 30s. In addition Moxon listed "Concave Hemispheres of the Starry Orb, which serves as a Case to a Terrestrial Globe of 3 inches Diameter, made portable for the pocket, 15/-" and "The English Globe, invented by the Earl of Castlemaine, 12 inches diameter,

40/- each". The Castlemaine globe, designed in 1679, consisted of a terrestrial globe supported on a short baluster stem rising from a flat circular foot of about 12 inches in diameter, engraved with celestial emblems, the rim marked as an hour circle. There is an example in University Library, Cambridge.

A Georgian price list issued in 1775 by Henry Pyefinch, 67 Cornhill, London, gives "New and Correct Globes" in five sizes, all in pairs: 17 inches diameter, £6 6s. od.; 12 inches, £3 3s. od.; 9 inches, £2 2s. od.; 6 inches, £1 11s. 6d.; 3 inches diameter pocket globes 9s. each.

Typical English terrestrial globes made from the 1590s until the nineteenth century were fitted into turner-made stands of hard wood, usually oak. Such a stand was composed of four or six baluster legs joined immediately above the small feet by flat cross stretchers. The stand might be made more stable by fixing a thin circular turned disc flat upon the surface of the stretchers which were then almost concealed. From its centre, or from the stretcher junction, rose a short stem slotted at the top to take a graduated meridian circle.

The legs supported a wide horizon circle or ring of turned wood, its flat upper surface covered with a printed ring, pasted on, showing the zodiacal signs, calendar, and names of principal winds. An hour circle might be attached to the north pole and a compass inserted in the base disc or a small one set in the horizon circle. Turned legs became more elaborate from the 1650s; the baluster was shorter with knops above and below. Swash- or twist-turning became fashionable from the 1670s until late in the century. Stretchers were also turned, extending from cubes placed between the legs and the feet to a central cube or cylinder supporting the post. A large globe of 26 inches or more in diameter would possess six or eight legs and the outer circumference of the horizon might be hexagonal or octagonal to harmonise. Uprights during George II's reign might be smoothly plain with a slight taper, and with capitals in gilded brass or ivory, but frequently upright and capital were turned in a piece.

No Georgian library was considered complete without a

pair of globes fitted into costly cabinet-made stands of mahogany. George II examples were supported on stands with finely carved cabriole legs and claw-and-ball or lion-paw feet, and with foliage enriching their expansive knees. Instead of being placed on a table, as was usual with turned stands, these were raised to eye level on well designed six- or twelve-sided plinths. Carving ornamented the outer rim of the horizon circle.

The tripod stand appeared late in the 1750s, three substantial legs supporting a short vase-shaped pedestal. From a brass cap fitted over the top of this branched four up-curving quadrants in gilded brass supporting a horizon encircled below with deep moulding. Between the feet might be fitted a compass on gilded brass brackets. In other examples the pedestals were six inches or so taller and the quadrants in carved mahogany. The mahogany tripod continued until the end of the Georgian period, plain with a smoothly turned supporting baluster.

Fashionable mahogany globe stands in the fourth quarter of the eighteenth century possessed vertical supports in the forms then favoured for chair legs such as the plain taper, smooth or fluted, with a spade foot, or the turned and fluted leg with swell foot. Castors were now fitted, sometimes with leather wheels. An apron of curved outline and enriched with carving was fitted beneath the horizon, between each pair of legs. From the 1790s the horizon might be encircled with a deep rim decorated with stringing or inlaid with checker ornament. The majority of early nineteenth-century globes, however, were fitted into stands of turned mahogany.

Terrestrial globes might now display the geological structure of the earth, indicate air currents, trade winds, monsoons, ocean currents, trade routes and lines of equal temperature. Papier-mâché globes were also made in which mountains were raised above the surface in disproportionate but fascinating relief-work.

Chapter Twelve

HANGING SHELVES

THE master craftsman, well-to-do shopkeeper and country yeoman of Tudor days valued among his domestic furnishings a set of framed shelves hung upon the living-room wall. Here were displayed a few luxuries, such as one or two Venetian glass goblets, a master salt in pewter, an earthenware vase, and treen turned from colourful woods. Silver was kept under lock and key in the master's bed-chamber.

Hanging shelves, joiner-made in oak, usually measured about 2 feet square and 6 inches deep with a shelf across the middle—three open shelves in all. The front edges of frame-work and shelf were trimmed with facings of oak, 2 or 3 inches wide. These might be carved with running scroll-work or other conventional pattern, inlaid with holly, bog oak or stained woods, or, more frequently, painted in bright hues with a touch of gilded design. The majority appear to have remained open at the back: others were boarded vertically and painted in colours, red, green and gold predominating.

Under the Stuart regime hanging shelves became rect-angular, measuring 30 inches high, 40 inches wide, and from 4 to 6 inches deep, and their facings were elaborately carved or inlaid with bone and ivory. The top might be more ornamental by the addition of two round-headed arches and a corbelled cornice. The central arch-joint was usually carried down to the shelf below, the double arcading forming an attractive frame for the display of the newly fashionable delft-ware dishes or plaques painted in cobalt blue. There are records of gilded hanging shelves carved in soft wood, making resplendent ornament against the wall-panelling. Entered in the inventory of Charles I's furniture at Hampton Court are "nine wooden hanging shelves, gilt, £9". A few years later Cromwell's goods included "one long black hanging shelfe for books" such as are to be seen in Dutch painting of the period.

Portable hanging shelves were made for convenience in transport. The cross-planks were cut with pierced lugs to pass through rectangular holes in the side pieces. Wedges were hammered into the lugs and the shelves held tightly in a single unit.

Hanging shelves were rarely inventoried during the second half of the seventeenth century (Ralph Edwards, *The Dictionary of English Furniture*) and few examples remain. It is probable that the old style continued in oak, the arcades being replaced by small cornice pediments late in the century. Fashionable use no doubt called for hanging shelves of gilded soft wood or walnut, types not capable of long wear— hence their disappearance. Hanging shelves are recorded in connection with the vogue for collecting oriental porcelains from the 1690s, but fixed shelves and brackets were soon preferred.

Books became more numerous from early in the eighteenth century and small numbers of these were kept on hanging shelves unless their owner could afford a bookcase. Such shelves hanging above a side table are seen in I. Cole's conversation piece "The Flute Player" pictured in *English Furniture Illustrated* by Oliver Brackett, and dating to about 1740. These are undecorated, consisting merely of planed shelves and sides without facings so that books could be removed easily.

Hanging shelves in mahogany designed in the Chinese taste and intended for the fashionable display of imported porcelain figures and vases date from the late 1740s. The demand by wealthy collectors increased during the 1750s as ornamental porcelain began to be made by English potters at Chelsea, Derby, Bow and elsewhere. Then, in November 1756, the King of Prussia, having occupied the town of Dresden, confiscated the stock of porcelain stored in the Meissen warehouse there and sold it to an

English group for £43,750, equal to more than half a million pounds today. During the next few years the London china-sellers were offering resplendent porcelains at considerably reduced prices.

This created a demand for handsome hanging shelves to display them. Thomas Chippendale in his *Director*, published mid-1754, illustrated eleven examples which he claimed to be "very light, but very strong". The sides and inner verticals were elaborately and delicately fretted with small versions of the Chinese railing associated with some Chippendale chairs and cut from the solid wood, rectangular or occasionally square. Each panel design throughout the piece might differ or all might be alike; in some instances the panels on each side differed from each other but matched the corresponding panels on the other side. Shelf edges were given fretted galleries to afford a measure of safety to the porcelain. Sometimes both upper and lower edges of the shelves were bordered with fretwork in either matching or contrasting designs. When the shelves were intended for books the galleries were omitted. Pagoda canopy pediments were fashionable and backs were boarded in with finely figured mahogany, an ideal background for the richly brilliant enamels and lustrous glazes of the porcelains.

Other hanging shelves were in three sections, the central tall and canopied, with one or two shelves, the others shorter, with or without a shelf. The top of each side section was either canopied or galleried. Width varied, but fashionably extended to about 3 feet: depth measured about 6 inches for porcelain and 9 inches for books. In some instances a spreading carved bracket beneath the centre gave pseudo-support, or there was one at each end, considered by Chippendale "to make good finishing". In his third edition of the *Director*, 1762, Chippendale reduced the number of china shelves and added designs of "shelfs for books". This confirms the fashion tendency away from porcelain display on open shelves to preservation behind glazed doors.

Ince and Mayhew in their *Universal System of Household Furniture*, 1759–63, illustrated several hanging shelves for porcelain including a design based on a shaped back board, with the shelves in graduated sizes and a pagoda pediment.

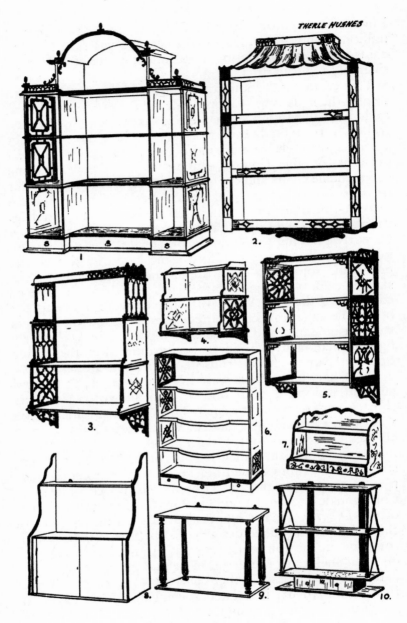

THERLE HUGHES

Fig. 4. Hanging Shelves

This probably created the fashion for simpler hanging shelves for books in three or four graduated tiers, the sides fret-cut in gothic or Chinese openwork, extending in curved outline above the top and below the bottom shelf.

In another fretted series the top shelf was galleried for porcelain; there were two book-shelves below; and beneath these a row of three shallow drawers, the top of their box forming yet another book-shelf. The sides might extend downward in the form of openwork scroll brackets. The top gallery or frieze might be ornamented with mock lattice work carved shallowly into the solid wood, or in the form of an applied fret against solid mahogany. This cut-card work, chiefly in geometrical patterns including simple curves, was a fretwork of mahogany glued upon the surface of a mahogany strip.

Mahogany fretwork hanging shelves might have the backboard extended above in the form of cresting and below in a harmonising shape: extensions might be pierced or solid. These are found with canted or right-angled fretted returns extending the length of each side, matching the gallery in width.

The mahogany used for the finest, most delicately cut of the hanging book-shelves was from San Domingo. Even when lavishly pierced this extremely hard wood was capable of standing strains impossible with other cabinet woods of similar thickness. By the 1770s softer, more easily worked mahoganies were used, but thicker, and with coarser piercing.

The open fretwork treatment of the sides of hanging book-shelves continued until the end of the century. The fashionable design demanded by the middle-class comprised several compartments, usually seven, three placed centrally one above the other, and flanked on each side with two. All uprights were fretted on their front surfaces and might be

HANGING SHELVES

1. Ten compartments and three drawers. Only the side verticals and the cresting rails are pierced.   2. With "Chinese" canopy. The shelves have pierced vertical borders for display of porcelain.   3. "Gothic" outlines to the pierced sides.   4. The simple two-tier style popular with more conventional piercing in the manner of glazed cupboards.   5. With irregular "Chinese" frets. The shelves have pierced corner brackets.   6. Hepplewhite style with simple repetitive pierced work.   7. Marquetry on sides and drawer fronts and a plain solid back. 8. Open shelves and deep cupboarding.   9, 10. Regency styles with a minimum of woodwork and no ornament.

enriched with marquetry banding. There were friezes above and a row of four veneered doors below.

Solid sides to hanging shelves of mahogany date from the the late 1770s. Hepplewhite in his *Guide*, 1788, noted that they "are often wanted as Bookshelves in closets or Ladies' rooms; they are also adapted to place China on", by which he indicated that the shelves should then be galleried. He illustrated an example, tall and narrow, with four shelves and a drawer below, and showed alternative ends, solid and fretted. In some instances side and drawer fronts were ornamented with marquetry in colourful woods: these were often designed *en suite* with a small side table above which the shelves were hung. Such shelves might be in satinwood with a backboard of the same wood. Another and wider design in solid wood was constructed with three shallow drawers at the base, two small cupboards flanking an open space immediately above, two book-shelves and a scroll pediment.

Thomas Sheraton's *Dictionary*, 1803, recorded that "small open hanging shelves are for books under present reading, and which a lady can move to any sitting room . . . they should also find a place in the tea room or breakfast room . . . they should be in mahogany or satinwood, banded on the edges of the shelves, which are seldom more than two in number, exclusive of top and bottom". Sides were carried up beyond the top and shaped in backward curves. Their recommended width ranged from 24 to 27 inches: large examples might be 5 feet wide and 9 inches deep.

A new style of hanging shelves was devised at the beginning of the nineteenth century. These were without sides, constructed from three plain shelves fitted into eight baluster-shaped colonettes headed by turned finials. Others had brass colonettes and there might also be brass cross-pieces at the ends of each shelf.

Regency hanging shelves were in mahogany or rosewood and enriched with brass, usually gilded. In these the sides might consist of several vertical brass rods and the shelves might be edged with cast and burnished brass ornament in a repeating design such as a row of small vine leaves. A variant was a brass lyre with strings at each end of each shelf.

Plate 25

Papier-mâché. (*Top left*) Vase decorated with realistic flower painting on green japanned background. The fittings are cast in a nickel alloy. (*Top right*) Pole-screen in paper ware, the panel painted in oils with an equestrian portrait of one of the royal princesses. (*Lower left*) Paper rack painted in the "Wolverhampton" style of decoration. This example is signed "Jennens & Bettridge," the notable Birmingham firm. (*Lower right*) Tip-up pedestal table decorated with a border of shell and gold bronze surrounding a flower painting in full colours.

Plate 26
Papier-mâché. (*Top*) Tray decorated with flowers and butterflies in gold on a black ground. Made by Shoolbred, Loveridge and Shoolbred, Wolverhampton. (*Below*) Paper rack from pulp-work panels, decorated in colours, bronzes and nautilus shell pearl.

Carved S-scroll ends of sturdy proportions might connect top and bottom shelves, the curve filled with three or four vertical brass rods. The majority of early nineteenth-century hanging shelves were made so that two shelves would each contain twenty-four volumes of novels.

Chapter Thirteeen

KNIFE CASES

WHEN Charles II presented the Duchess of Portsmouth with a dozen each of golden knives and forks with matching handles, he inaugurated a fashion that continued in ever-growing dimensions throughout the Georgian era. Formerly it had been customary for a visiting guest to bring his own knife and fork: by 1820 a host's table silver might number more than a thousand pieces.

Matching sets of knives and forks in silver brought in their train standing cases specially designed to contain a dozen of each, placed vertically with handles upward. A cursory glance was enough to tell the owner if one were missing before the cases were locked and carried to the butler's pantry or strong-room. Spoons were soon added to such sets and accommodated in the cases.

Table silver was not changed for each course of the meal: the pieces were washed in the dining-room under watchful eyes at a cistern provided for the purpose. Lady Grisell Baillie in her *Household Book* 1743 copied out the directions she gave to her servants. These included a comprehensive list of rules to be observed in the dining-room: ". . . never let the dirty knives, forks and spoons go out of the dining room, but put them all on the box that stands for that use under the side table", and "As soon as a glass is drunk out of, range it directly in the brass pail which you must have there with water for that purpose".

The earliest pictorial record of a standing knife case appears in the manuscript of Randle Holmes's *Academy of Armory*, 1649, where two pen and ink drawings illustrate such a case open and closed. These, reproduced in *The Dictionary of English Furniture* by Ralph Edwards, show cases with flat lids sloping downward to the front with widely canted front corners. Knife cases at this time were covered with leather or shagreen or japanned in colours and gilded.

The earliest knife cases appear to have been in deal covered with black leather which might have gilded borders and be tooled all over with scale ornament, leaving reserves for stamped motifs. They were further enriched with silver mountings and feet. Linings were of deep red velvet edged with braid worked from gold or silver wire; mid-eighteenth century examples might be lined with red chamois leather. In the Earl of Shrewsbury's inventory taken in 1726 such a case contained twelve each of knives, forks and spoons all gilded.

Shagreen-covered knife cases date from the William and Mary period. In 1706 Kersey's *Dictionary* defined shagreen as "a sort of rough, green leather: as a Shagreen Case". Such a case was specified by Peter Faneuil when in 1738 he ordered furniture and silver plate from London, including "a shagreen case with a dozen new knives and forks of handsome silver handles, and the best blades you can get, for my own use, with room in the case for a dozen spoons". The case was required to be lined with red velvet. Shagreen was prepared from the untanned hides of horses and camels. After soaking in water and de-hairing they were cut into suitable sections and sprinkled with goosefoot seeds (*Chenopodium album*). These were covered with hard felt and pressed into the skin, thus producing a granular finish: the skin was then dyed, usually green with sal ammoniac and copper filings: less frequently it was coloured red with cochineal, or black with logwood and lampblack.

In the collection of Sir Ambrose Heal is a trade card issued in about 1760 by "John Folgham, Shagreen Case-Maker, Opposite the Castle Inn, Wood Street, London", announcing that he "Makes and sells all kinds of Shagreen, Nurses, Fish Skin, and Mahogany Knife Cases". Illustrated is an open knife case displaying two dozen knives and a dozen each of forks and spoons. The knives and forks have pistol handles and are arranged in six rows of six: the spoons are accommodated in the curving front in rows of five, four, two and one.

The nurse-skin and fish-skin were less costly than shagreen which they closely resembled. The nurse-skin came from the rough-skinned shark known as the sea dog or dog fish: the fish-skin was taken from the spiny skinned ray fish (*Raja fullonica*) caught in the northern waters off England and Scotland. After being dried the skin was glued to the knife case and the spines removed with a file and smoothed with shave grass and dyed. Undyed this so-called shagreen acquires a high polish by rubbing with oil and rotten-stone.

Knife case carcases were almost invariably of red deal, a wood defined by Sheraton in his *Cabinet Dictionary*, 1803, as deriving "from Deel, Dutch for a part, quantity or degree of. Hence fir or pine timber being cut into thin portions they are called Deels". In early examples the bow fronts of knife cases were shaped from thin wood whilst hot and these, like the flat surfaces, were veneered, usually in mahogany. Both carcase wood and veneer required to be properly seasoned to avoid shrinkage and subsequent cracking of the veneer.

Knife case making became a specialist branch of the cabinet-making trade, both tools and manipulation being distinctive. Thomas Sheraton in his *Cabinet Maker and Upholsterer's Drawing Book*, 1791–3, pointed out that knife cases were "not made by regular cabinet shops" and recommended his cabinet-maker readers to obtain them "from John Lane, No. 44, St. Martin's-Le-Grand, a maker of ladies' work boxes".

The veneer itself was hand-cut from the log at veneer-cutting establishments by pairs of expert veneer cutters working in the pit and providing, six, seven, or eight veneers of unvarying thickness from each inch of wood. This was sold to cabinet-makers and knife case makers in its rough state. In 1806 the *Annual Register* recorded the introduction of a new method of cutting veneers by means of steam-driven saws cutting several simultaneously at a speed that vastly reduced costs.

Knife case veneering was an occupation requiring considerable skill. Straight-grained veneer was selected for flat surfaces except the top, which with the bowed or serpentine front, was covered with curled veneer. It might be laid with the grain either vertical or horizontal. The carcase units

Plate 27

Claw tables. (*Top left*) Mahogany with almost square top, its gallery pierced and carved with scrolling acanthus foliage; the fluted columns rise from a baluster carved with upspringing and descending acanthus leaves. The cabriole legs are carved on the knees with acanthus leaves and have claw-and-ball feet. (*Upper right*) Mahogany with octagonal top, the gallery fretted. The support is cup-shaped in its upper section with a pear-shaped baluster below carved with acanthus foliage on a pounced ground. The three incurved legs have scroll feet. (*Lower left*) In pearwood with plain turned column and scroll legs on castors. About 1690. (*Lower right*) Mahogany with pierced gallery on triple open baluster pillar; cabriole legs with scroll feet. The "bird-cage" beneath the top shows the wedge which may be withdrawn, allowing the top to be lifted from the pillar.

Mahogany claw tables. (*Left*) Claw reading-table with a plain column issuing from a carved baluster; cabriole legs carved on the knees with cabochons and foliage; scroll feet with castors. Made by William France for the first Lord Mansfield, Kenwood House, Hampstead. (*Right*) Top scalloped and elaborately carved with a border of flowers and foliage; with a "bird-cage" beneath, a carved column and baluster, and cabriole legs with claw-and-ball feet. About 1760.

Plate 28
(*Left*) Drum table in rosewood on concave tripod legs. (*Right*) Mahogany, the gallery pierced with a medallion and key fret design and the rim below carved with C-scrolls; the stem pierced and carved as three conjoined C-scroll supports; the legs carved below the knees with small pendant foliage medallions and terminating in scroll club feet.

made of deal were thinly coated with fine glue and allowed to dry. Bending the veneer to fit snugly against the curved front of the knife case body and lid was a complicated process. The underside of the veneer was roughened and it was then soaked in heated size to make it pliable. This was placed over the carcase unit, close adhesion being secured by means of a heated caul. This was a board shaped as a counterpart of the contour to be veneered. The heat kept the glue sufficiently fluid for any surplus to be pressed out from the edges as the clamp screws were tightened. The glue gradually set hard and the caul could be removed with safety late on the following day. A sheet of paper between caul and veneer prevented sticking.

Veneer, cut a little larger than the area of the surface to be covered, was glued to flat-faced carcase units by means of a veneering hammer. This was a wooden block measuring about 3 inches square and 1 inch thick, with a strip of iron plate inserted into one edge. This straight edge was pressed upon the veneer with a zig-zag movement, from the centre outward, thus forcing out all surplus glue. The veneer surfaces were finally stained and then polished with dog-fish skin, beeswax, and shave grass.

The interiors of veneered knife cases were as meticulously finished as the exteriors. The box and lid rims were finished with cock beading to disguise the join of veneer and deal carcase, and the base and lid were edged to match. The early boxes were divided into many small square or rectangular compartments, partitions extending to the base. These were arranged in tiers to facilitate the removal of knives and forks by their handles, which were supported by the partition rims: spoons were inserted with their bowls upward. Compartments and lid interiors might be lined with velvet, or with baize, which was afforded some protection against moths by a panel of cedar between the baize and the wood of the lid.

Mountings might be of silver or of gilded brass, silver being the more frequent until the 1770s but seldom used after the opening of the nineteenth century. The lid was fitted with a central plate-ring by which it was opened: on each side was a lifting loop hinged to an expansive plate which might be fretted or engraved. A hasp was attached to the front of the lid, its lock, with an escutcheon matching the side plates, fixed to the front of the box immediately below. Box locks with link plates and inlaid keyhole escutcheons date from the 1780s onwards. The back corners of the case were protected with fretted corner-pieces and mounted on claw-and-ball feet: there was a third foot, with an ornamental fret at the front centre. Feet were rarely fitted after about 1780. Early plates and escutcheons were hand-sawn from the metal sheet; later they were cast, and finally might be stamped. Hinges were so designed that they held the lid sufficiently open for knives and forks to be removed easily.

By the mid-eighteenth century standing knife cases might be made in pairs; in sets of three, with the centre case, containing spoons, shorter than the other two; and, towards the end of the century, in sets of four.

Knife cases from the 1760s reflected the current taste for lighter-hued exotic woods. Satinwood, unstained and polished, might be decorated with marquetry, such as green-stained husk patterns, or might have swags painted on the panels, but the less costly knife cases of mahogany remained supreme.

Corners of mahogany knife cases might be inlaid with herring-bone stringing, and textile and leather linings gave way to polished interiors. The partitioning now consisted of a panel pierced with apertures in shapes designed to hold the knives, forks and spoons firmly in position without division of the box into numerous compartments extending to the base. Each aperture might be edged with fine chequer inlay. The lid interior of polished wood was usually inlaid with a boxwood and ebony star or an oval or semi-circular fan, frequently shaded, within a panel formed by a checkered line of the same woods. These decorations were bought from marquetry specialists ready for insertion into the veneer. The sloping outer surface of the lid might be inlaid with the owner's coat of arms in woods dyed to the appropriate heraldic colours. Gillow's letter book under the date 22nd January 1776 describes such a knife case as of "fine mahogany within and without, strung with a little inlaid work around each knife, fork, etc., and also on the inside".

By the mid-1770s fashionable knife case fronts displayed a serpentine contour—a convex curve flanked on each side by a fluted pilaster. These were soon less expensively replaced by two plain concave curves, the knife case front being veneered in three sections, the wide convex curve and the two narrow concave curves, joins being concealed by stringing, soon to be applied to all visible corners and edges. Cross-banding in yew or light-coloured woods edged with ebony or fine checkered stringing outlined the front panel and the lid. Early in the period there might be a ring plate on the front of the lid directly above the inlaid keyhole escutcheon, but mountings were soon abandoned.

Early in the nineteenth century the bold front curve of the standing knife case narrowed and flattened, with a convex pilaster each side. Soon the front was flat with an incurving pilaster at each side, or narrow concave corners. The front panel and lid were cross-banded and stringing was in white holly and ebony.

Thomas Sheraton in his *Cabinet Maker and Upholsterer's Drawing Book* illustrates a standing knife case with a boldly convex front and incurved corner pilasters, inlaid with holly or coloured woods. The centre panel was cross-banded and japanned with small flowers, the lid decorated with an inlaid patera.

Japanned knife cases were made throughout the period, at first in japanned or lacquered wood ornamented with oriental scenes in gold. They were made in pairs, one box containing a dozen knives, the other a dozen forks. The lid was flat-topped and opened on the slant to display two tiers of knife or fork handles held in velvet lined compartments edged with braid in gold or silver wire. They were fitted with gilded hasps and their locks had extensive escutcheon plates. From the middle of the century knife cases of japanned copper were made, their fronts boldly curved and decorated with colourful floral devices in gilded borders, or with landscapes and figures.

Knife cases in painted enamel copied the form of the mahogany type, with sloping lid and serpentine front. The example in the Ionides Collection is painted with coastal views in full colour, minor decoration of dainty flower sprays being repeated on the tapered cylindrical knife and fork handles contained within the case. Silversmiths made knife cases in similar form, but the number existing suggests that demand was small. The surfaces of such a case were smoothly plain with a coat of arms engraved on the convex front or on the lid.

Vase-shaped knife, fork and spoon cases were introduced in the 1770s, following the vogue for classic urn shapes. They were sold in pairs to stand at the ends of the sideboard, or in sets of three, the shorter vase being reserved for spoons. When Sophie von la Roche visited London in 1786 and inspected the showrooms of the cabinet-maker Seddon at 151 Aldersgate Street, she commented with approval on "three vases to hold spoons, knives and forks. These pieces are extremely tasteful in ornamenting a dining room".

Hepplewhite's *Guide*, 1788, referred to vase knife cases as "usually made of satin and other light woods". Many, however, were made in mahogany, body and cover decorated with lines of vertical stringing concealing the seam joints of the veneer. Some attractive examples are found in chestnut and sycamore. The design usually has a round foot and stands upon a square plinth which may have a bracket foot at each corner. Frieze and plinth are sometimes fluted.

Because of the practical difficulty in hinging circular lids, the dome cover of the vase-shaped knife case was supported on an extending shaft rising from the centre of the body. This might be of cast brass working on a slide principle and held in position by a spring, or might be a tube containing a close fitting inner lining, enabling the cover to be raised as required. The knives, forks and spoons were placed concentrically in a circular rack fitting into the rim of the vase, the rows tiered sometimes to the number of five.

The late Georgian vase knife case degenerated into an elongated four-sided sarcophagus type raised on four paw feet of gilded brass. The body might have canted corners and the front panel might be cross-banded with satinwood or sycamore.

Chapter Fourteen

THE wealthy Georgian home welcomed its guests into a spacious hall and up the grand staircase to the staterooms on the floor above. More often than not the whole gracious tone of the reception was set by the brilliance of the many-candled chandeliers magnificently framed in glazed lanterns. Due regard has been paid by collectors to such multi-branched chandeliers, but comparatively few, perhaps, appreciate the quality of design and craftsmanship involved in the lantern frames that protected the candles in such draughty situations and the finely-clad guests below them from drips of candle-grease. So obvious and alarming were the possible dangers of any fault in the construction of such massive furnishings that their creation was the work of specialists, from the 8-foot-high frame of brass and glass over the staircase to the individual candle-sockets in the smallest lanterns around the walls.

Hall lanterns usually burned candles of bleached wax rendered hard-textured by a basting and rolling process. These had wicks of twisted, unbleached Turkey cotton, considered most resistant to the high temperature of melting wax. On formal occasions candles of costly unbleached beeswax were favoured for the brilliance of their flame and the fragrance of the melting wax. A thin film of bleached beeswax gave the candles a white appearance.

Some Georgian lanterns were enormous. Sir Robert Walpole hung in the stone hall at Houghton a gilded copper lantern encasing an eighteen-candle chandelier. Horace Walpole sold this to Lord Chesterfield in 1750 and replaced it with an even larger lantern acquired from Lord

Cholmondeley. More normally the hall lantern would be designed to accommodate five or six branches without crowding.

The majority of the lavishly designed pendant lanterns of the 1740s and onwards were in brass. Thomas Chippendale in the third edition of *The Gentleman and Cabinet-Maker's Director*, 1759–62, illustrated eleven examples of "Lanthorns for Halls and Staircases" in elaborate rococo designs, cast in brass from wooden moulds. Some were six-sided and others square with corners recessed. The scale of inches included with the drawings shows their heights to have approximated 4, 6 and 8 feet.

The plate glass panels might be concave, convex or flat, and fitted into grooves so that they could be removed easily for cleaning. Until the early 1770s they were imported from Paris although they were cut, ground and polished in London. One side of the lantern was hinged to form a door so that the snuffer-boy could snuff the burning candle-wicks when required. A lantern was commonly hung so that this could be done from the staircase although no insuperable difficulty was involved in lowering the lantern and chandelier by means of cords and pulleys.

Lantern making in brass was a specialist craft. It was essential to construct the basic frame so that no distortion could occur whilst it was suspended from the ceiling, and to ensure that the neck was capable of carrying the weight of metal and glass below without risk of fracture. The head was elaborately designed. In a royal palace or government building it was often shaped as a crown. A coronet might be used, according to the owner's rank, or a vase-shape enriched with acanthus leaves. Within the ornamental head were the swivel and pulley. The lantern was suspended from a ceiling hook by means of four colourful cords, a gigantic tassel concealing the double pulley. In 1750 Mrs. Delany in a letter to the Duchess of Portland mentioned that she was "diligently engaged in working an ornament to hide the pulley of the chandelier".

Hall lanterns were fitted with four or six short feet such as plain balls, turned knops, inverted vases, or pineapples. Chippendale's designs show elaborate scroll feet. In the more ornate patterns each corner support might be extended downward to form a foot, or an applied motif might terminate in a hoof or a dolphin's head.

Lanterns of gilded brass were costly objects. At Hampton Court Palace, hanging at the foot of the Queen's Great Staircase, is an octagonal lantern in gilded brass headed by a large royal crown, the base encircled with terminal figures. This was installed in 1729 by Benjamin Goodison of the Golden Spread Eagle, Long Acre, at a cost of £138. Among the trade cards illustrating Sir Ambrose Heal's *London Furniture Makers* two of the 1760s refer to brass lanterns. Peter Langlois, of Tottenham Court Road, announced "Branch Chandeliers and Lanthorns in Brass", stating that he was a specialist in ormolu work, and Jonathan Fall, at the Blue Curtain, St. Paul's Churchyard, announced that he supplied "Brass Lanthorns and Arms". George Seddon, the celebrated cabinet-maker, operated a brass-making, finishing and gilding department at his Aldersgate Street factory, and no doubt he produced brass lanterns.

Ince and Mayhew, who published their *Universal System of Household Furniture* in 1762–3, illustrated lanterns closely resembling those of Chippendale and noted the combination of lantern and chandelier. They captioned elaborate acanthus scrollwork and foliage as "Raffle Leaf", and illustrated staircase lantern lights "designed to fix on the handrail". Robert Adam designed lanterns of which no duplicates were made. An octagonal lantern made in 1770 for Harewood House was of gilded wrought iron with applied cast ornament. The uprights were formed as female terminal figures and the frieze and base were encircled with honeysuckle ornament.

Lanterns containing one or two candles were fixed to the walls of staircases and passages giving just enough illumination to light the way. These were cabinet-makers' productions with frames of walnut or mahogany and gilded mouldings. The lantern back was lined with a reflecting mirror plate, and the front and sides were glazed. One of the side panels, usually the right, was hinged to give access for snuffing and cleaning. In some instances the sides and front of a wall lantern hinged open as a single entity. At first the top was open and occasionally is found with a metal smoke shade curving forward from the back. This collected soot from the smoke and was wiped clean every day. Alternatively the back panel was arched above the cornice and fitted with a projecting hook suspending a smoke shade of flint-glass.

The wooden base was protected by a metal plate and to this were soldered one or two cylindrical candle-sockets fitted with flint-glass sconces obtainable from glass sellers at about twopence each. In some instances the wood base was covered by a mirror plate and a portable saucer-shaped candlestick with a ring handle was placed upon this, sometimes in silver. It was essential that the candle should be securely anchored: if it slipped or warped the glass might be broken with the hazard of fire. The socket was therefore deep. A typical example in mahogany made for Hampton Court Palace in 1720 measures 2 feet in height, 12 inches wide and 9 inches deep. Thomas Moore, cabinet-maker, of St. Martin's Lane, London, in 1734 charged the "Honourable Counsellor Rider for 5 large hansome Wallnuttree Compass Side Lanthorns with Plate Glass Backs, and fixing Do £10.0.0".

Wall lanterns by the mid-eighteenth century displayed the rococo mood in mahogany with acanthus leaves or shells as the central motifs of undulating arched cornices. The side panels for the most part were widely canted, and carved double C-scrolls might support the candle platform. The mahogany might be enriched with applied motifs in gilded brass or in carved deal, gesso-coated and gilded. At Norfolk House, St. James's Square, for example, over the doorway at the foot of the grand staircase was a pair of mahogany wall lanterns, carved and gilded. These were surmounted by golden eagles with outstretched wings.

Later in the century the fashionable mahogany wall lantern was rectangular with a downward taper. In 1790 Lord Spencer bought "2 Long square Handsome taper Copper Lanthorns with Neate Pearsed and Cheased taper Fret Borders" for £26 5s. od.

Corner lanterns were cabinet-made, too, in walnut and mahogany, plain or slightly carved. In this design the back consisted of reflecting mirrors with shaped tops set at right

Plate 29

(*Top left*) Mahogany tea-table with tray top, octagonal and with a wavy rim, the pedestal fluted and the tripod carved with acanthus on claw feet. (*Top right*) Mahogany tea-table, the edge of the top carved in cyma outline and the vase-shaped base supported by a carved tripod ending in claw-and-ball feet. (*Lower left*) Mahogany tea-table with shaped top made to tilt; the spiral turned shaft with vase-shaped base rests on a carved tripod. (*Lower right*) Satinwood and mahogany table, its turned shaft supported by four concave legs. Late eighteenth century.

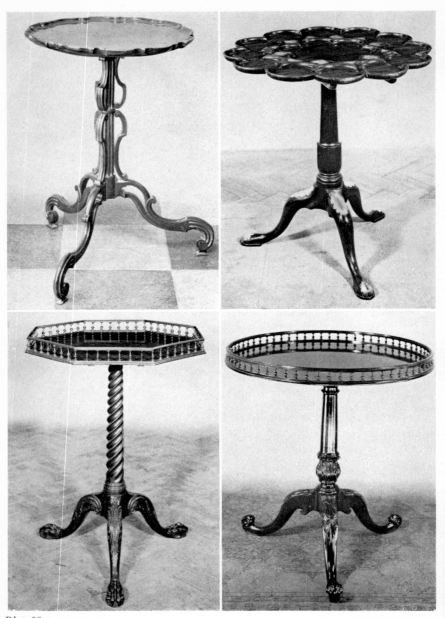

Plate 30

(*Top left*) Tea-table in mahogany, the top with a raised and moulded edge, the fluted stem with three pairs of S-scrolls. (*Top right*) Mahogany dessert table, the top cut from the solid wood; the knees and feet of the tripod decorated with gilded silver plate. Mid-eighteenth century. (*Lower left*) Mahogany tea-table with octagonal top and spindle gallery; the shaft spirally fluted. Mid-eighteenth century. (*Lower right*) Tea-table with spindle gallery, on plain column carved with acanthus leaves harmonising with the cabriole legs on scroll feet.

angles. The typical arc-shaped front was enclosed by a convex glazed door and the cornice double arched. The open-topped lantern of this type usually burned a single candle, just enough to light a dark corner. Others were of copper with mirror panels and base. The upper cornice might be ornamented with a fret gallery or, from about 1780, with one of cast lead. The top was enclosed, with a low dome, leaving a small aperture for ventilation.

Georgian wall lanterns included globes of blown flint-glass dating from about 1740 onwards. Double annealing in a tunnel lehr then made it possible to toughen glass to resist the heat emitted by a single candle; earlier this would eventually have cracked it. The open moulded globe was attached to a deep candle-socket rising from a curved branch of scrolled ironwork or cast brass. From a matching bracket above hung an expansive smoke-shade of glass. In the *Dublin Journal*, 1750, the Round Glasshouse advertised "hall lanthorns in glass for 1 to 4 candles; cut and plain barrel lanthornes; globe lamps; all in the newest fashioned mounts now used in London".

Many wall lanterns were made in japanned metals. These were often thought desirable for positions where they might be left unattended for long periods. They copied the cabinet-makers' shapes but with plain surfaces. The backs were set with reflecting mirrors until the early 1740s when the interiors were polished. This marked the japanner's change from ordinary sheet iron to tinned plate. Colours acquired a high brilliance on this base and lost their former tendency to flake away. Many of these were the productions of John Baskerville of Birmingham, the frames often japanned to represent either red mahogany or tortoiseshell. Japanned metal was also used for hanging hall lanterns. The description of Strawberry Hill, 1782, records that "in the well of the staircase by a cord of black and yellow, hangs a gothic lantern of tin japanned, designed by Mr. Bentley and filled with painted glass". The designer was probably Thomas Bentley of Chelsea, Josiah Wedgwood's partner in the manufacture of ornamental wares. Coppersmiths made lanterns, too: to save the labour of polishing most were passed through a process of "browning".

Metal-framed lanterns were also fitted to staircase newels. Six such lanterns adorned the grand staircase of Kensington Palace for more than a century. The accounts dated 1729 described them as "12 inches square and 17 inches high, with a shade over each, and two flat sockets for candles". No examples of such newel lights are known to remain.

Portable lanterns stood on side tables in long passages, at bends of staircases, and in small rooms where occasional light might be needed. Some of these lanterns were elaborately worked in walnut or mahogany and examples have been noticed resembling the cases of giant bracket clocks. These were mirrored on back and base, glazed on three sides, and provided at the top with a circular ventilator. The candle might burn in a socket or a saucer candlestick. Matching sets of these might equip an entire house. In some specimens dating to early in George III's reign a gilded brass frame was fitted with a wide inner border of painted enamel work.

Towards the end of the eighteenth century hanging lanterns tended to be replaced by open-flame oil-burning lamps. Existing drawings by Robert Adam show them to have been designed for "staircases, halls, passages, lobbies". Colza oil was generally used, the wicks requiring a negligible amount of pricking in place of snuffing.

Chapter Fifteen

PAPIER-MÂCHÉ FURNITURE

EARLY Victorian drawing-room elegance found perfect expression in furniture and minor accessories of papier-mâché. Luscious carvings, restless wallpapers, light-subduing figured lace curtains, all demanded the positive, assertive vigour of its glossy surface, its nearly-gaudy ornament, its emphatic outlines. But so closely is the work associated with Victoriana that it is essential to appreciate how many of the processes had been developed in late Georgian days.

For half a century the manufacture of furniture in tough, heat- and moisture-resistant papier-mâché was an important and profitable industry in Birmingham and Wolverhampton. Chairs, sofas, sofa and tripod tables, pole screens, needlework stands, teapoys, even pianos, all constructed without framework, might naively glow with oil paints, iridescent pearl, and glittering metallic powders. Bedrooms might scintillate with brass and papier-mâché beds, flamboyant wardrobes, and glossy dressing tables.

The earliest of this brilliantly resplendent furniture displayed a surface finish suggestive of oriental lacquer and was hand-made throughout from specially prepared paper by processes patented in 1772 by Henry Clay, 19 Newhall Street, Birmingham. Clay exploited his patent to the full and amassed great wealth, finding employment for more than six hundred people. Throughout the hundred years of its manufacture Clay's invention was known as paper ware and until 1861 was subject to a heavy paper tax. Clay's patent specification included furniture, but little is known to have been made by him. The earliest reference to an actual piece so far noted is recorded in the Strawberry Hill Accounts for 1778

127

where reference is made to a writing table of "Clay's ware" designed and decorated by Paul Sandby. Tables and screens were enriched with costly oil paintings by well-known artists. A set of console tables made for Queen Charlotte were ornamented with paintings after Guido Reni by the Wolverhampton artist Edward Bird, then practising at Bath.

Paper-ware furniture was a luxury production until late in the Regency period when small pieces began to be produced on a commercial scale and were illustrated in merchants' pattern books. Tip-up tables, pole screens, and teapoys were made, all with pillars rising from expansive feet.

The less costly "papier mâché japan furniture" dates from 1836 when Richard Brindley of Birmingham patented a method by which he pressed one-piece shaped blanks and rolled thick panels from non-taxed rag pulp. These hard blanks or units were assembled directly into furniture. The validity of the patent was challenged by competitors and was quashed in 1842.

The two types, Clay's paper ware and Brindley's pâpier-mâché japan ware, were not known indiscriminately as papier-mâché until the 1860s. They are easily distinguished from each other. Paper ware has a flat, absolutely smooth surface, is lighter in weight than the pressed ware which is brittle by comparison and less frequently found in mint condition. The glossy surface of the pressed ware reveals a texture when held in an oblique light.

Paper ware furniture was made from clear, unsized greyish-green paper composed of clean linen rags and resembling modern blotting paper, but with a thicker, tougher texture. Sheets cut to a suitable size were saturated with flour-glue paste and laid over a tallowed metal mould modelled to the shape of the unit required. Four or five sheets were laid and hand-pressed against the mould, a process which also forced out superfluous paste. The paper, still on its mould, was then stove dried at a temperature of about 100° F. and afterwards coarsely rasped so that the next sheet adhered firmly. Another group of four or five sheets was then laid and the process repeated until the required thickness was reached. The blank was then water-proofed by soaking for several hours in linseed oil and spirits

Plate 31

(*Top left*) Pearwood joint stool with turned baluster legs and shaped underframing. Mid-eighteenth century. (*Top right*) Oak joint stool with legs of fluted baluster form, splayed back and front for stability. About 1600. (*Left centre*) Oak stool with canework and bobbin turning, japanned black with decoration in gold and colours. Late seventeenth century. (*Centre right*) Stool of English walnut, legs with faceted "mushroom" cappings, scroll feet and central stretcher. (*Bottom left*) Walnut stool upholstered in velvet; legs with faceted mushroom cappings, ending in volutes. Carved stretcher. 1690s. (*Bottom right*) Walnut stool with cabriole legs and unusually expansive curved corner brackets.

Plate 32
Stools. (*Top left*) In gilt gesso with cabriole legs and turned stretcher. (*Top right*) In walnut with masks and acanthus leaves carved on the cabriole legs and paw feet. Early Georgian. (*Left centre*) In dark Spanish mahogany with drop-in seat and carved seat rail, the cabriole legs carved with lion masks and with claw-and-ball feet. (*Centre right*) Mahogany in the Chinese taste with column legs and guttae feet. 1760s. (*Bottom left*) In walnut with drop-in seat, the legs tapering to club feet, and turned stretchers. (*Bottom right*) Walnut with drop-in seat and incurved seat rail, the cabriole legs carved with escallop shells and terminating in claw-and-ball feet.

of tar, and re-stoved for three hours at a higher temperature. This so hardened the paper that it could be treated as wood and planed, carved or filed. In the case of hollow-ware, after the second stoving the paper was cut either vertically or horizontally and the core removed.

The units for a piece of furniture were assembled by skilled cabinet-makers and then coated with a mixture of tar varnish and fine lampblack. When dry this was painted over with tar varnish and stoved for twelve hours. Crimson, green or blue was obtained by adding colour to the varnish instead of lampblack: the adhesive used for fixing the sheets was also coloured.

A fine surface finish was secured by applying several coats of hard, transparent varnish, each stove-dried for twenty-four hours—twice as long for furniture of high quality. This process was repeated again and again until the surface was suitable for decoration. Afterwards the ware was again stoved, coated with transparent copal varnish, and stoved for the last time. It was then sent to the polishers, whose bare hands dipped in water produced the beautiful glass-like lustre which made new paper ware so desirable.

Brindley's papier-mâché japanned ware, described by the Jury of the Great Exhibition as "a mass of barbarous splendour", was much less costly than paper ware. It was this material that was fashioned into papier-mâché chairs and other shaped furniture. The thick sheets, known as blocks, from which the furniture units were made, came from the press wet and easy to mould. Sheets never warped or split although sometimes measuring as much as 8 feet by 3 feet. If intended for use as flat panels they were dried at once in a hot room. When required for shaped work they were placed, whilst wet, over solid iron moulds and hand-modelled into position, every part being forced firmly against the metal. Over this was placed a hollow mould of sheet iron, interior and exterior conforming to the shape of the solid mould. This was covered with another wet block and the process repeated four or five times, each layer forming a separate blank. The whole was then lifted to a press table and pressure was applied, gradually increasing over a period of about four hours. The blocks were then so dry that they retained the shape of the mould. From 1847 they might be steamed whilst in the press, thus securing denser material of unvarying section throughout. The rough-surfaced whitish-brown blanks were removed from the press and taken immediately to a drying room.

The hard, dry blanks were given additional strength by soaking them in linseed oil long enough to secure complete penetration. After drying in a japanning oven they were ready for the cabinet-maker, japanner and decorator. Simulated carving for attaching to furniture was made by a similar process.

Ornament on early papier-mâché furniture consisted mainly of allegorical, oriental and sporting scenes painted in oils, enriched with surrounds in gold, or all-over designs composed of flower, foliage, butterfly and insect motifs. The gold was applied either in the leaf or as powder strewn over a tacky surface to produce high-light effects on fine work. Two qualities of gold were used: either pure metal or low-carat. Gold paint was never used.

The popularity of gold ornament prompted the development of glittering bronze powders used in a range of lighter colours consisting of finely ground brass, copper, zinc, dutch metal and other colourful alloys. Trees, for instance, might be painted in green bronze with shadows in blacklead. This was an invention patented in 1812 by Thomas Hubball of Clerkenwell, but not widely used until the late 1820s.

The radiance of gold and bronze on the glossy lacquer-like surface brought about the development of chinoiserie ornament on paper ware, principal exponent being Joseph Booth of the firm of Jennens and Bettridge, Birmingham. His style, dating from about 1825 and soon copied by others, consisted of using impasto or relief gesso, made from gold size and whiting, for raised portions of oriental designs, such as pagodas and junks, temples and towers, bridges, mandarins, and so on. His pole screens with panels decorated in this way made him celebrated. From about 1830 pearl ornament was introduced in trees and the like in association with gold tracery. Palm trees with alternate fronds of pearl and gold had a fashionable vogue.

Pearl shell inlay was patented in 1825 by George Souter

of Jennens and Bettridge. The early pearl ornament was made from laminae of four types of nautilus shell ground to a thinness of one-hundredth of an inch, so that they could be blown about like paper. Under the terms of the patent the pearl was outlined and cut into design by means of strong acid used in association with a waxy acid-resisting paint. Extremely delicate work was produced in this way—far more delicate than anything possible by the saw-cutting and press-cutting methods which were soon adopted to evade the patent.

Although termed inlay, the pearly ornament was actually stuck to the wet japanned ground. When all the pieces were arranged, repeated coatings of tar varnish were applied, filling up interstices and gradually concealing the pearl. The entire surface was then polished with rotten-stone, revealing the pearl and preparing for the gold and painted decorations.

Larger, more sturdy flakes of pearl might be used from about 1840 to represent roofs and domes of temples and pagodas. The surface might be slightly convex, rising above the surrounding japan and catching the light from different angles, providing contrasts in iridescence. Bowls and baskets of flowers in pearl date from about 1845 onwards.

A new method of decorating with bronze was evolved in the mid-1840s, known as the Wolverhampton style. This was specially suitable for portraying effects of contrasting sun and shadow, a proportion of the design being brush-painted in oils. The various coloured bronzes were applied with swabs in a special design consisting of a fragment of leather attached to a fine thread passing through the hollow of a quill so that it formed a tiny pad at the tip. The tool was capable of producing the most delicate touches.

Outdoor scenes were given brilliantly sunny skies, and ruined buildings showed vividly against sombre masses of trees. Stone walls and pillars of church interiors were bathed in a golden glow streaming from gothic windows. The rare silvery bronze made from aluminium appeared on moonlight studies and as cloud edgings from about 1860. Henry Perks, celebrated for his skill in blending bronze powders, produced the finest work in this medium.

Oil paintings were seldom applied to furniture until George Neville, of Jennens and Bettridge, evolved a jet-black japan in the early 1830s. This was the first English-made black japan to be free from the tendency to fade to an unpleasant green.

The demand for black japanned paper ware displaying competent oil paintings was immediate and the work included pole screens, teapoys, table tops and so on. Established artists are known to have worked anonymously, earning high fees for painting original pictures to commission. Expert copyists soon abounded in Birmingham and Wolverhampton, reproducing efficiently painted versions of old masters. Some of these men concentrated on the work of a single artist: William Davis, for instance, evolved a style closely reproducing that of George Morland.

Contemporary paintings were copied without compunction until the passing of the Registration of Designs Act in 1842 which prevented unauthorised copying. Landseer and Wilkie were notable sufferers from piracy of their works by the japanners. Artists were now paid to give permission for their work to be copied. Birket Foster, for instance, licensed the Walton firm of Wolverhampton so that their artist George Hickey might reproduce his landscapes and country scenes. Works of past artists continued to be reproduced without fee, such as Cipriani, Kauffmann, Barker of Bath, Singleton and Hamilton.

Large firms, of course, employed master artists whose technique was suitable for speedy copying. If such copies appear meticulous and bleakly efficient rather than inspired it must be remembered that decorators worked fourteen hours a day, for a wage of thirty to fifty shillings a week. When daylight faded, their only illumination might be evil-smelling open-flame whale-oil lamps giving no more light than a couple of modern candles. The Walton factory, for instance, did not instal gas until the late 1840s.

It is sometimes suggested that the papier-mâché trade had become obsolete by the mid-1850s. In 1856, however, the British Association published a report stating that fifteen manufacturers were then operating in Birmingham, that the demand for large articles of furniture and chairs was increasing, and that shipbuilders were placing orders for large ornamental panels for ships' cabins.

Chapter Sixteen

PILLAR-AND-CLAW TABLES

THE mahogany claw table was one of the most elegant, shapely little pieces of furniture in the early Georgian drawing-room. Yet it was the direct descendant of candle-stands and tables designed for homes so primitive, and floors so rough, that stability could only be ensured with a three-footed, design. The basic shape, consisting of a small table top supported by a pillar resting on three equally spaced feet, is found in innumerable early candle and rushlight holders. Indeed, the majority of remaining pieces of seventeenth-century claw furniture are stands for candles, although in some instances these have been altered since into tables. Nevertheless, English claw tables have a history of at least a thousand years.

The eleventh-century Cotton MS. in the British Museum illustrates a small round table with a spreading base supporting a central pillar. Claw tables are noted from time to time in Elizabethan inventories, such as "ij Wainsket pillar tables" at Marketon in 1545, and an illustration of two octagonal tables with carved pillars and claw feet appears in the Lumley inventory, 1590. The Earl of Northampton's inventory, 1614, records "a little round table upon a colombe painted with watchett [a pale blue colour] and silver. XIIIˡIVᵈ".

By early Georgian days claw tables in glowing mahogany were proving ideal for the silver and oriental porcelain of the tea equipage, matched by claw kettle stands where again safety demanded that slender elegance should be combined with rigidity. By the 1740s the drawing-room banquet was ideally served by such tables which could be set out with all the sumptuous desserts of the period (see Chapters 6 and 18). In the centre would be piled a four-tiered pyramid of stemmed salvers in flint-glass, parading an array of sweetmeats in their individual glasses. Dishes of fruits, cakes and other confections would be arranged around the centre-piece, circular depressions sometimes being sunk into the mahogany of the table top to accommodate the dishes. By 1750 claw tables of simple design might be ordered in matching sets of four, six or a dozen for the banquet dessert.

The earliest remaining examples of claw tables date to the late seventeenth century, the claw consisting of three decidedly angular S-scroll feet, square in section and with a definite shoulder or corner to mark the meeting of concave and convex curves (Plate 27). These were let into the base of the pillar. By the early eighteenth century the curves of the claws had become more flowing, leading to the perfection of line found in early Georgian round section cabriole or ogee legs poised on claw, claw-and-ball, paw, scroll, or dolphin-head feet.

"A mahogany scollop'd Tee-Table on a claw" entered in Sir William Stanhope's furniture inventory of 1733, is the earliest reference so far noted to a claw table in mahogany. Five years later the Duke of Atholl bought a mahogany claw table with a galleried top from John Hodson, a cabinet-maker of Frith Street, Soho, London. This was illustrated in *Country Life*, 18th November 1949. Trade cards consistently refer to claw tables by name throughout the eighteenth century. John Hodson's card, issued before 1744, illustrates a claw table with a turned pillar and plain claw, a claw reading desk, and a tea urn stand with a carved pillar and turned claw. Sir John Hall in 1759 paid Young and Trotter of Frith Street £1 15s. od. for "a fine Jam* Mahogany Tea Table with Scolloped Corners 39 × 30 on top Pillar and Claw, feet with castors". John Trotter was upholder to George II. Ince and Mayhew in their *Universal System of Household Furniture*, issued in parts from 1759 to 1763, illustrate "Three very neat designs for Claw Tables".

Early imports of mahogany were costly and used only for fine furniture. It was extremely hard, exceptionally close of grain, with a rich red colour and displaying little or no figure. So difficult was the wood to work with the cutting steel then available that tools required continual sharpening and renewal. Carving carried out on such mahogany—known as San Domingo, Spanish and Jamaican—retains its edges as sharply crisp today as when they left the workshop. The actual manipulation of the tools gave to the wood a high polish, making finishing treatment unnecessary.

The table tops and supporting pillars, save in exceptional circumstances, were rough-shaped in the lathe. The foot-operated pole lathe, such as any cabinet-maker of the day might possess, was incapable of coping with hard San Domingo mahogany. The split or sawn logs were sent, therefore, to professional wood-turners operating throw lathes powered by boys who, when experienced, turned the driving wheels with unerring uniformity of speed. In this type of lathe the wood revolved with a continual swift forward motion so that the tool did not need to be lifted intermittently from the work as with a pole lathe. The huge girth of San Domingo mahogany enabled slices to be sawn from the log and shaped into one-piece table tops. Special lathes were evolved so that pie-crust and scalloped edges could be cut and shaped mechanically.

The removal of duty on imported timber in 1733 led to the introduction of a wider variety of cabinet woods, including Honduras mahogany or baywood. This wood was easier to work than San Domingo mahogany, being less heavy, with a straight, open grain. As it was lighter in hue it was dyed a vivid red to emulate the earlier wood, its grain filled by coating several times with gum lac. It was finished by rubbing with powdered brick dust and linseed oil laboriously applied with a beaver pad. This gave it a fine hard-wearing polish which has darkened through the years. The lower costs involved influenced the design of claw tables from the 1740s, wood-turners now entering into competition with cabinet-makers by producing simplified versions of claw tables.

The earliest mahogany claw tables seemed to grip the floor. The claw was formed of three widely outspreading, boldly incurved legs terminating in scroll feet and measured about half the height of the table (Plate 27). The claw supported a short, stout pillar consisting of a deep cup-shaped upper section measuring about 5 inches in diameter joined to a pear-shaped baluster below by means of a plain, narrow, spool-shaped motif. Upper and lower sections might be carved in high relief with acanthus foliage, and similar decoration might extend to the upper surface of the claw. The pillar was thick enough to give adequate support to a table top which might be encircled with a hand-cut open-work gallery, strongly built in sections and lacking the elegance of later work.

Such sturdy claw tables in mahogany were the first of a long line in this wood. Those displaying elegance of design, fine carving and skilful craftsmanship were the work of cabinet-makers and were made until the 1780s. Tremendous quantities of plainly turned and mechanically gadrooned and fluted claw tables were made by the wood-turners between the 1740s and about 1850, chronological changes in design, manufacturing techniques and quality of mahogany enabling them to be grouped in several well-defined categories.

The pillar, also termed a column or central shaft, was usually of baluster outline, rising from the strong base-block in the centre of the claw. Its pear-shaped lower end was carved in a wide range of designs, among which were included acanthus leaves, serrated leafage, scrolls, cabochon ornament and gadrooning. This continued upward in a slender column which might be carved to match or encircled with deep vertical flutes. Turners shaped such pillars from working drawings supplied by cabinet-makers, or provided stock patterns. Large firms such as those of Chippendale and Seddon obviously would establish adequate turning facilities in their own workshops.

When the wood-turners included this branch of furniture-making among their long list of productions, the cabinet men designed pillars impossible to reproduce by mechanical means. These were recognisable at a glance and included pillars consisting of hollow balusters and others in which the pillar was constructed from three open-work scrolls extending its full length and suggestive of flying buttresses, giving particularly delightful play of convex and concave curves. In another design a cluster of engaged columns with an ornamental band mid-way and sometimes intended to imitate bamboo, would rise from a polygonal block. Pillars themselves might be octagonal throughout their length, each surface closely carved.

The turners, obviously, found it convenient to continue the baluster tradition with mechanically cut gadrooning and fluting of the pillar. A trade card issued in about 1755 by Thomas Hollinshed, Drury Lane, and now in the collection of Sir Ambrose Heal, lists the range of claw furniture made by the wood turners. Hollinshed announced that he made and sold "all Sorts of Turnery Goods in Mahogany, Walnuttree &c., viz. Dumb Waiters, Claw Tables, Fire Screens, Tea Kettle Stands, Candle Stands". All these were made with claws and it is interesting to note that such furniture was still being made in walnut.

From the 1780s pillars were almost invariably turned in various forms of the baluster. Early in the nineteenth century the introduction of steam-driven woodwork lathes and finer quality cutting steels speeded production immensely, lowering the cost and thus increasing demand. From about 1820 such tables might be French-polished.

The claw itself was constructed from a central block and three out-spreading leg units. The pillar was set vertically into the claw-block by means of a strong well-fitting dowel and so skilfully was this done that even today it is difficult to detect where block and pillar join. Before fixing the pillar the legs were dovetailed into the block. A flaring tenon was cut on the end of each leg and three matching mortices cut vertically into the block. When inserted they formed an interlocking joint fitting so tightly that they cannot be pulled apart except in one direction. The downward pressure of the pillar and table top ensure rigidity.

Early claw legs were in cabriole or ogee form. In San Domingo mahogany they were cut individually from thick planks, but with the advent of Honduras mahogany it proved less expensive to slice sections from a baulk shaped to the desired silhouette. They were then finished by hand-tooling.

Cabriole legs at first terminated in upward scroll feet

with soles beneath providing flat surfaces for the floor. Ornamental carving harmonising with that on the pillar extended well down the upper surfaces of the legs. Claw-and-ball feet soon made their appearance on these tables, adapted from the oriental design of a dragon's claw grasping a pearl. Eagles' claws are often noted on mahogany claw tables (Plate 28). The claw-and-ball foot is not included in the fashionable designs illustrating Chippendale's *Director*, 1754, and was seldom used in this connection after the 1760s. Early claws were vigorously carved and the lower half of the ball extending beyond the grasp of the claw was cut away to give stability to the table. Other feet found on claw tables are the lion's paw, hoof, and, from about 1750, the French dolphin head.

The snake's head or club foot was used by the wood-turners on account of its simplicity in manufacture and low cost. This continued in use throughout the period of claw tables. In some early examples such legs were elaborated by carving the knees with simple motifs such as acanthus leaves.

Claw tables had lost much of their distinction by the 1780s. Although baluster pillars remained well-proportioned, there was a tendency to economise in wood and to spoil the design with sagging, sprawling legs. The cabriole curve was superseded on fashionable claws by a concave curve reeded on its upper surface and terminating in a more or less round foot. Late eighteenth-century work might introduce a little pointed pendant finial beneath the pillar, a feature of some Queen Anne furniture. The popularity of these tables increased in the early nineteenth century in a light-weight series, the curve of the legs being reversed.

The tops of mahogany claw tables might be circular, rectangular, square, octagonal, scalloped, or irregular. Galleries encircled the tops of some early ones, a feature fashionable until the 1770s. It is often said that the galleried tables were for displaying porcelain, then highly expensive: this is most unlikely owing to the portable nature of such tables. China tables were rectangular with four legs as illustrated in Chippendale's *Director* and other pattern books. The earliest galleries fitted to claw tables were cabinet-makers' productions, consisting of hand-carved, outward-sloping perforated work cut from the solid wood. These were succeeded by hand-pierced vertical lattice work, and by the middle of the century less costly fret-cut galleries in patterns severely formal and geometric, the frets being cut from three layers of wood, glued together in different ways of the grain, and enclosed in frames of solid mahogany.

Spindle galleries appear to date from the late 1730s and to have been originally a cabinet-maker's enrichment. These galleries consist of a row of turned baluster spindles sometimes interspersed with oval motifs which might be used as handle-grips in carrying the table fully loaded into a room. In some instances the rims above and below the spindles were encircled with simple hand-carved motifs. The turners sometimes added a gallery of spindles to a claw table from the early 1750s, and thereafter this feature seldom appeared on cabinet-makers' specimens.

The vast majority of claw table tops were circular and sunk in the lathe so that a raised border resembling moulding encircled the edge. These were made until the close of the eighteenth century. In the 1730s appeared the pie-crust or scalloped table top with the raised edge shaped in a series of curves and often enriched with carved motifs. At first these table tops were entirely hand-carved by the cabinet-makers working in San Domingo mahogany. Such work is not difficult to distinguish from the pie-crust tables made by the wood-turners from the 1750s by means of a special wood-cutting machine which sank the centre and scalloped the edges.

The table top was fixed to the pillar in early work by means of an applied turned collar into which the pillar was screwed. By 1740 the top might tip into a vertical position when not in use; from 1740 it might revolve, and, according to J. C. Rogers, from 1755 it was designed so that the withdrawal of a wedge-shaped cotter permitted the top to be lifted from the pillar. The result was the introduction of the well-known "bird-cage" claw table. Two bearers extending almost the entire diameter of the table top were screwed to the underside. Between them, under the centre of the table, was the open "cage", made by joining two squares of mahogany at each corner by short turned baluster spindles. The bearers were bored to take pivots projecting from the corners of the square cage roof. A spring was fitted to the top, engaging into a socket in the cage, to secure the top of the table firmly when horizontal.

The top of the pillar was tapered so that it passed through a hole of similar diameter bored through the floor of the cage. A vertical slot was cut through the tapered section of the pillar and a wooden wedge-shaped cotter inserted through the slot made the top rigid. The table top with cage would revolve if required on a bearing surface cut below the taper of the pillar; it could be tilted vertical by pressing the spring catch, or could be lifted from the pillar by removing the cotter.

Chapter Seventeen

STANDS FOR BASINS

WASHING the face and hands in the bedroom at a specially constructed device is a 500-year-old custom in England. Tudor gentry used a metal basin fitted into an iron stand and filled from a laver of water suspended above. The laver was a two-spouted cauldron of silver, pewter, copper or brass hung by a loop handle from a bracket over the basin. By tipping up one spout the water was poured through the other spout into the basin. This was the fashionable washing equipment in the bedroom for about two centuries.

Metal basins with accompanying ewers were also used, standing on a small table. Earthenware of the period was unsuitable, as water could not be left in it for long without seeping through. Stoneware was impervious to water but there is no evidence that it was used for this purpose.

A special stand to accommodate the basin did not appear as a piece of cabinet furniture until the mid-eighteenth century. The earliest printed reference so far noted is in the third edition of Chippendale's *Director*, 1762. Here plate LV illustrates three "Designs for Bason Stands" drawn by Chippendale and engraved by Mathias Darly. The first consists of a tripod foot, an open-work column supporting a short hexagonal pedestal with an acanthus leaf calyx and, emerging from this, three ogee supports holding a carved basin ring. Of the second pattern Chippendale comments: "it hath Four Feet, and Four Gothic Pillars and an Arch on each side." The basin holder is flat, of square outline with clipped corners. The third pattern was the forerunner of the fashionable basin stand for the next quarter century with drawer, wash-ball container and water bottle shelf.

These wash basin stands of mahogany were designed to take advantage of improvements in Staffordshire earthenware manufacture. For the first time the potters were producing earthenware rendered non-porous by being fired to a biscuit, dipped into liquid lead glaze, and refired. The result was a highly lustrous and uniform white surface which could be enamelled in colours or painted in blue under the glaze.

The Chippendale design had evolved by 1770 into the well-known standard wash basin stand, constructed by the cabinet-maker from eleven units of mahogany tenoned together. Beginning at the base, there were three cabriole legs, carved at the knees, often with claw-and-ball feet, but more usually plain with pad feet. These supported a triangular platform or plinth, each side fitted with a carved or plain frieze, and with a circular depression in the centre for the water bottle. From this plinth rose three short turned pedestals continuing as scroll-shaped supports bearing a second triangular unit that contained two small drawers, one below the other. On top of this was a hollow, globe-shaped container for a wash-ball, its finialled lid carved or smoothly plain. It has been thought, mistakenly, that this was intended for a wig or as a container of hair powder, so that the name of powder stand has been wrongly applied. From the corners of the drawer-box three more scrolls supported the circular basin ring, flat beneath and rounded on top, or pulley shape. Height always approximated 31 inches.

Clean water was contained at first in a long-necked bulbous-shaped bottle about a foot tall. This stood in the depression sunk into the lower triangular plinth. Bottle and basin might be painted with matching designs, in blue under the glaze or in a range of enamel colours. Earthenware ewers containing a plentiful supply of water would appear to have been a nineteenth-century innovation, for Thomas Sheraton noted in 1803 that the lower plinth should not be

STANDS FOR BASINS

1-3. 1750s and 1760s. Fig 1 is a Chippendale design without a soap ball holder. Fig 2 is a "Gothic" design. 4-8. 1780s and 1790s, associated with Hepplewhite and Shearer. Fig 5 includes a mirror and enclosed front. 9-12. 1790s and 1800s. Fig 9 is a Sheraton design with a cistern and tap and a lead-lined drawer. In Fig 10 the back folds forward and the sides fold down to mask its purpose. Fig 11 is a Sheraton design with a cistern and tap, a sliding tambour front and a waste pipe from the basin to a vessel in the cupboard.

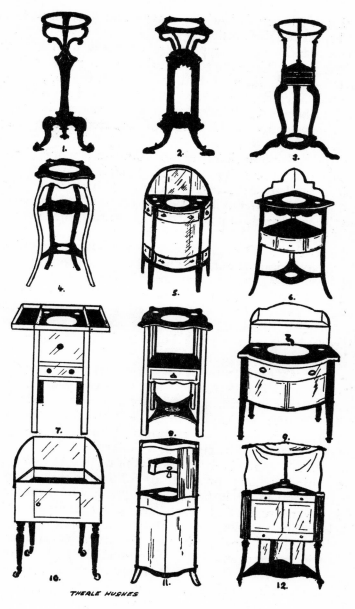

THEALE HUGHES

Fig. 5.   Stands for basins

less than 13 inches below the drawer-box "to allow sufficient height for the bottle".

Basin stands of this type were enriched with carving until the 1770s. Then the scrollwork was left plain and was oval in section, the wash-ball container being omitted in favour of an earthenware receptacle decorated *en suite* with basin and bottle. On several examples examined the upper drawer was lined with thick lead foil, omitted from modern copies.

Basin stands were also made in colourful japanned beech from the early 1760s. Thomas Chippendale himself in 1768 invoiced Sir Edward Knatchbull with "a very neat Bason Stand Japan'd Green and Gold. £2.10.0". Less costly examples were made of painted deal by the furniture factories from the 1780s.

Chippendale's design consisting only of a flat basin holder, pedestal and tripod stand, with no accommodation for water bottle or wash-ball, was not successful for examples are rare. It was re-introduced, however, at the end of the century, four slender turned legs with a curved X-stretcher replacing pedestal and tripod. The basin ring was cut square with clipped corners from a thick board and fitted with a deep frieze.

By the early nineteenth century stands of mahogany were severely plain. The depression in the lower platform was turned to fit the foot rim of a small ewer. The lower and upper scrolls with the blocks that held the drawer-box were cut from single lengths of soft mahogany. The bowl ring was smoothly turned in the shape of a pulley.

Square basin stands were also fashionable. At first these were cabinet-makers' productions following the Chippendale style and in finely figured mahogany which might be solid or veneered. The flat top, measuring about 21 inches wide by 16 inches deep, was cut with circular holes to receive a wash basin and a pair of hemispherical wash-ball holders, usually in pewter with wide horizontal rims. The front frieze was in the form of two rows of shallow dummy drawers with hinged loop handles of gilded brass. Fourteen inches below was a shelf, square with clipped corners and a fretted or plain gallery. This was attached to the straight

Plate 33

(*Top*) Writing-box of filigree paper work in imitation of carved ivory. Late eighteenth century. 10½ inches × 8¾ inches × 3¾ inches. (*Below*) Circular stools in walnut, late seventeenth century: (*left*) on scrolled legs with turned cross stretchers and central finial · (*right*) with turned swelling legs and curved cross stretchers.

Plate 34
Tea canisters and chests. (*Top*) In satinwood with lock escutcheon of hand-worked silver, struck with the hallmark of William Grundy, London, 1758. (*Below*) In mahogany with silver mounts; the canisters bear the hallmark of Pierre Gillois, London, 1772.

rectangular legs by means of short scroll stretchers extending from the corners. Chippendale illustrated a typical example showing the looking glass raised from a slot in the back and held up with a spring catch to form a splash-board.

The common square basin stand, so termed by Sheraton and usually a factory production, dates from the early 1780s onwards. This was backed with a shaped splash-board, and the underside of the bowl concealed below a deep apron. Legs were straight and usually square with splayed front feet and sometimes carved to match the reeding on contemporary bedposts. Below the centre was placed a square shelf forming the top of a box containing one or two shallow drawers. A second square shelf or stretchers might be fixed immediately above floor level, in which case the drawers were raised to a position at least 14 inches above the floor.

Sheraton, in 1803, defined such a stand merely as "a piece of furniture much in use and as generally known", and advised that they should be made from Honduras mahogany in sizes ranging from 13 inches to 15 inches square and 34 inches high.

Basin stands with closed tops became popular early in the nineteenth century, simpler versions of the earlier toilet tables containing a multitude of fittings. These were square with the space between the basin and drawer-box enclosed by a tambour cover or cupboard door. Beneath might be a single drawer extending the full width and depth of the piece and in some instances there was a second cupboard below. Edges were reeded to harmonise with the fluted legs and fittings such as hinges, castors, and knobs to the tambour, drawer and cupboard were in brass.

Some designs included a cupboard above the basin, tambour fronted to enclose a small water cistern which was lead-lined and had a hinged cover. A tap from the cistern filled the basin and a waste pipe emptied it into a bucket in another cupboard below.

Square basin stands in mahogany, covered and uncovered, were made in a multitude of patterns from 1817 until the 1830s. Plainness and simplicity were the rule as work of cabinet-makers' quality became less frequent.

Corner basin stands with their rounded fronts of finely figured mahogany occupied a minimum of space in small bed- or dressing-rooms. They came into use during the early 1780s, typical productions of the furniture factory. The basin fitted into the flat top shelf, and a pair of circular holes contained wash-ball and sponge bowls. The design books of Hepplewhite, Sheraton and Shearer all illustrate corner as well as square basin stands, indicative of their widespread popularity. The two straight sides against the walls were fitted with splash-boards, their gracefully curved outlines avoiding the dullness of a flat top. In the nineteenth century the upper corner might have a small shelf for a water carafe and tumbler. A deep frieze around the quarter-circle curve of the top concealed the lower part of the bowl. This frieze at first was cut with a wavy edge harmonising with the splash-board curves.

A rounded box for drawers was fitted about halfway between the frieze and the floor, three small drawers in a single line being usual until the late 1790s. By the nineteenth century a single drawer extending the full width of the piece was the standard fitment, or there might be a single narrow drawer in the centre. About 13 inches below the drawer-box was a bottle shelf cut from flat veneered wood, with three stretchers connecting with the legs and so arranged that the bottle was towards the front and easy to grasp. This shelf was sunk with a circular recess for the water bottle, but from late in the eighteenth century the bottle, and eventually the ewer, stood within the basin, and the lower shelf was left smooth. Sheraton in his *Drawing Book*, 1791–3, illustrates two corner basin stands, one with three drawers and a bottle shelf with a shallow circular recess. The other has, at floor level, a quarter-circle shelf of the same size as the top and without feet. This is the earliest record of a basin stand lacking a bottle recess.

The front legs at first were rectangular, of the same thickness as the splash-board, and splayed forward against the angle of the wall. Later and more frequently legs were square and tapered, usually splayed towards the foot, and occasionally with spade feet.

The frieze had become straight-edged by the opening of

the nineteenth century and the space above and below the drawer-box might be enclosed with a pair of convex doors. Below this cover there might be a row of three narrow drawers or more frequently a single wide drawer. These were in mahogany and might be ornamented with small panels of inlay and two-colour stringing. This unit stood upon slender turned legs, often reeded, extra stability being secured by the placing of a fourth leg at the centre of the front when it was more boldly curved than usual.

By 1810 the basin commonly stood upon a flat upper shelf, the filled ewer being placed within it. The capacity of basin and ewer had been increased considerably by 1820 and the basin stand was no longer large enough to carry it—hence the introduction of the washstand with its marble top.

Chapter Eighteen

STOOLS

WILLIAM COWPER in his poem "The Task" gives a sketch of the evolution of the stool:

> ". . . stools were then created, on three legs
> Upborne they stood. Three legs upholding firm
> A massive slab, in fashion round and square . . .
> At length a generation more refined
> Improved the simple plan; made three legs four,
> Gave them a twisted form vermicular,
> And o'er the seat, with plentious wadding studd'd,
> Induc'd a splendid cover, green and blue,
> Yellow and red, of tap'stry richly wrought,
> And woven close, a needlework sublime."

Chests and stools were the most numerous articles of domestic furniture in English living-rooms until the sixteenth century, a single chair being set for the master of the house, his symbol of authority. This custom continued to some extent into the Stewart period. The great chamber at Gilling Castle, Yorkshire, in 1594 contained twenty-eight stools and only one chair: when the next inventory was taken thirty years later the stools numbered thirty-five and there were two chairs. At the earlier date the dining parlour contained buffet stools, forms and cushions and no chairs: by 1624 three chairs had been introduced. This, however, may be regarded as an extreme example: before the end of the sixteenth century a well-established merchant or shop-keeper would usually possess at least one or two chairs in each major room of his rambling house. The half dozen or dozen buffet stools in his dining chamber might be supplemented by several chairs or to some extent replaced by forms made more comfortable by cushions. Thus Ralph

Plate 35

(*Left*) A collection of late-eighteenth-century tea-caddies including oval, octagonal and fruit forms. (*Upper right*) Mahogany tea-chest of serpentine shape with ormolu foliage handle, its lid enclosing three divisions, the canted angles and borders carved with foliage, scrolls and pendant husks and terminating in scroll feet. (*Lower right*) Shagreen-covered tea-chest with mounts in hallmarked silver. 1750s.

Plate 36
(*Top left*) Tea-canister set with ivory plates in gilded brass mounts. (*Top centre and right*) Ivory
tea-caddies inlaid with ebony lines; shield-shaped silver name plates. Late eighteenth century.
(*Centre left*) Oval satinwood and marquetry caddy. (*Centre*) Satinwood tea-chest with medal-
lions of burr walnut. (*Centre right*) Urn-shaped tea-caddy with ivory finial and key escutcheon.
(*Bottom*) Three oval tea-caddies in mahogany enriched with oil painting.

Willey, gentleman, of Houghton in the Syde, Co. Durham, in 1584 had three long forms, eight buffet stools and two chairs in his "hall house". John March of Redworth in 1590 had two chairs and five stools in the hall, but twelve cushions, presumably for a form which was a wall fixture.

Sir Thomas Ramsey, a former Lord Mayor of London, at the time of his death in 1590 possessed about three dozen joined stools. In the "Newe Parlour" was "1 drawing joyned table wth a frame and xviij joyned stooles" valued at 33s. 4d., and in the hall were a further eight joined stools and two wainscot forms, valued at 21s. The new parlour also contained "2 stooles of needlework, 4s." and "4 olde greene stooles, 5s." as well as "3 chaires and 2 chaire stooles of crimson velvet, 6s. 8d." A single joined stool was priced at one shilling.

Joined stools were so called to distinguish their better quality from common turnery or carpentry at a time when turners, carpenters and joiners were separate City Companies. Carpenters might make only rough furniture of nail and socket construction without use of glue. Joiners possessed the monopoly for making "all tables and stooles of wainscote, walnutt, or other stuffe, glued, with frames, mortresses, or tennants, or any other articles of furniture that require to be dovetailed, pinned or glued".

The earliest style of English stool might have a round, square, or triangular top with three outspreading plainly turned legs, capable of standing firmly upon the usual uneven floors. The humble versions were roughly and heavily made from any easily worked wood available but the only survivors today are in hard oak. The demand for three-legged domestic stools continued until Victorian days.

Stools for formal occasions were of the trestle type, constructed from thick planks of sawn wood. Most existing examples are in oak. Lord Lumley, however, possessed fifty-seven stools of inlaid walnut as well as 118 of wainscot: pearwood, elm, yew, birch and beech examples have been recorded. The splayed end supports had buttressed edges and each was divided into two feet by an ogee arch close to ground level. They were united by a pair of deep underframes extending beyond the legs and usually pierced.

Wooden pegs or dowel pins held them firmly in slots cut into the supports. The seat, measuring about 22 inches wide and a foot deep, was smoothly rounded off or moulded at the edges.

Stools with four legs braced together by stretchers are illustrated in illuminated manuscripts of the fifteenth century. These were joined or joint stools, made by joiners using the mortice and tenon technique. The seat might tilt very slightly forward, and the forward and backward splay of the legs increased rigidity upon the floor. A sideways splay would have made the stool less convenient for its major purpose at the dining table. From the mid-sixteenth century the deep frieze rail of wavy or scroll outline might be carved with the fruiting vine or some similar pattern or less deeply ornamented with scratch work. Four strong plain stretchers were fitted 2 inches or so above floor level. Legs at first were plainly turned columns, left square for the seat rail and stretcher joints, and from the mid-sixteenth century might be in baluster form carved with channelled grooves or flutes. The seat might be made to hinge upward and the frieze enclosed below to form a box.

When numbers of stools were used in a room they formed a matching set. Dining-room stools were so designed that when not in use they could be ranged beneath the long table with their tops outward, and supported by the near stretcher: legs of table and stools matched. Their plain wooden tops might be covered with embroidered cushions. Sir John Harrington in 1596 noted that in every merchant's hall stood "easy quilted and lined formes and stools".

It is difficult to distinguish between many Elizabethan joint stools and those of the first half of the seventeenth century, although in the later work the style and treatment of carved features sometimes provide a clue, such as in the arcading on the underframing, or carved leaves in a series of arches and semi-circles, or scrolls and medallions. Legs might be turned in plain columnar form with ball feet, or as slender balusters or in ring-and-ball pattern. The width of the top increased from about 18 or 20 inches to as much as 27 inches. Squabs or pads lightly filled with horsehair or tow were sometimes used as cushions and tied to the legs, but more frequently the seat was covered with a thin pad of hide fringed with cut leather. Chairs and stools were covered *en suite*.

Joined stools are sometimes known to collectors as "coffin" stools because a pair of such stools formed a convenient rest for a coffin awaiting the funeral. Pepys noted this in his *Diary* July 1661: "My uncle's corps in a coffin standing upon joynt-stools in the chimney in the hall."

Inventories prove the existence of costly padded stools covered with embroidery worked in colours and gold thread. Henry VIII introduced these luxury stools from Italy and only the wealthy could afford them. The Earl of Northampton possessed many. The furniture in his "Dininge Chamber" consisted of "a high chaire, a low chaire, two high stooles, and one low stoole of clothe of gold, the ground maidenheare with fringe and tassels of golde lined with damaske watchett [pale blue] and maidenheare xiiij^{li}; 6 highe stooles of russet velvett frindged iiij^{li}; a long table of walnuttree xlv^s". The "Wynter Dyning Chamber" was furnished with "one highe chaire, two highe stooles, two low stooles of wrought purple velvet sutable iij^{li}; one lowe stoole of black velvett imbrodered with a rowe of slippes of silver x^s; a court cupboard of walnuttree and a square table of walnuttree xvj^d; eight high stooles of tawny velvet with cases liij^s iij^d". "Stooles in their cases" is a term frequently found in records of the period and not always correctly interpreted: the cases were loose covers to protect the embroidered tops from the effects of sunlight which would quickly fade some of the vegetable dyes then in use. This, of course, was one reason for the popularity of gold and silver thread work. Low chairs and low stools were designed for women's use, Henry VIII's inventory of 1547 referring to this custom: "one lowe stoole for a woman of wood covered with crymson cloth of gould tissue and reysed with crymson vellvet upon velvett with redd sylke".

James I introduced to the English court the privilege of the tabouret which gave to designated ladies the right to be seated in the presence of their monarch. The upholstered stools provided were of the low variety. When the Constable of Castile was entertained at Whitehall in 1704, he sat upon "a tabouret of brocade with a high cushion". The cushion raised him to the same height as the king who sat on a chair at the head of the table. In the reign of Charles II tabouret etiquette extended into the homes of nobles and merchant princes on ceremonial occasions. Count Lorenzo Magalotti in his *Travels Through England*, 1669, observed that when Cosmi III, Duke of Tuscany, visited Wilton "there was prepared for his highness, at the head of the table, an arm-chair, which he insisted upon the young ladye's taking; upon which the earl instantly drew forward a similar one, in which the serene prince sat, all the rest sitting upon stools". Tabouret etiquette was strictly observed at the English court until the mid-eighteenth century.

Tabouret stools are thought to have been round-topped. Ordinary upholstered stools of the early periods were rectangular, the wooden frames resembling those of joined stools, but constructed from soft timber such as beech, and painted and gilded. This appears to have been the standard form until about 1660.

Upholstered stools from the Restoration until the mid-eighteenth century became progressively more elaborate in design. Until the end of the seventeenth century they were most usually in walnut but frequently in soft woods enriched with colourful paints, gilding or silvering, and japan work. These harmonised with their new chair styles introduced from the continent. At first legs and stretchers were swash-turned—the well-known barley-sugar spiral—with cane seats set in rails which might be plain, convex or carved. In the early 1670s legs and side stretchers might be of the cube-and-ball variety with elongated ball feet.

These became outmoded during the 1670s by stools with scrolled legs and upholstered seats. The forward curve of the legs might be carved with one, two or three acanthus leaves. Feet were also scrolled. Turned stretchers extended between front and back legs, and these were centrally joined by a single cross stretcher. Elaborately carved scrolled stretchers back and front, serving merely as ornament, were set between the upper curves of the legs. By the late 1680s such stretchers tended to be deeper than formerly, extending almost to the seat rail and carved with intricate open-work.

Seats were thickly upholstered and covered in the period's fashionable velvets and figured damasks.

William and Mary stools were characterised by the X-shaped stretcher, straight or serpentine, moulded on the upper surface and flat beneath, with an upright vase finial concealing the central join. Legs might be of tapered pillar style, or octagonal balusters; they might be fluted, plain, or faceted pear-shapes, faceted mushroom balusters, cupped, perhaps, with gadrooning, or any number of individually designed forms. The feet were usually knurled—in inward turning moulded scrolls. Ornamental stretchers continued to be fitted back and front until about 1695, lavishly carved in open-work scrolls and foliage. The upholstery was now carried over to conceal the seat rails. Walnut continued to be the favourite wood, but gilded and silvered beechwood were fashionable also.

Stools of the early eighteenth century—a period too extensive to be contained in Queen Anne's reign—were influenced by chairs imported from Holland. Cabriole legs with hoof or club feet became fashionable, at first narrow at the knee and bordered with carved C-scrolls. There were square cabrioles too with square club feet. Bracket extensions might be carried beneath the seat rails and later became a standard feature. At first the legs were united by plainly turned end and central stretchers and the feet might be scrolled. Chair-making developments by 1710 prompted stool-makers to carry the tops of the legs into the seat rail, forming part of it and thus rendering superfluous the strengthening under-stretchers. Cabriole legs were then made wide and stouter, often hipped around the corners of the seat frame. Claw-and-ball feet were introduced and continued until the mid-eighteenth century together with club feet: hooves were occasionally featured. Knees were customarily carved with escallop shell motifs, but other designs in low relief were used.

Seat rails, usually deep and moulded on their top edges, had to be made deep enough to be tenoned into the blocks left at the tops of the legs. When an upholstered drop-in seat was used, the upper half of each seat rail had to be reduced in thickness to receive it. Additional strengthening of the joints between seat rails and legs was obtained by screwing in triangular blocks which also helped to support the loose seats.

The majority of Queen Anne stools were of walnut throughout; many others were japanned in green and gold; and there was a demand for a combination of walnut and gilded gesso.

These styles continued virtually unaltered until the 1720s when mahogany began to be used. The high duties levied on imported timber until 1733 limited the use of the weighty new mahogany, however, and as far as possible it was veneered over native woods such as oak and beech. Until the mid-eighteenth-century walnut continued to be used more extensively than mahogany. The dense growth of the early mahogany offered splendid opportunities for carving, in contrast to the flat surface effects of walnut veneers, and on stools this was particularly conspicuous in the deep, vigorous carving of leg knees. Motifs continued to be dominated by escallop shells and pendant foliage and husks, but variety included lion masks with and without acanthus leaves below, and some legs were carved with scales and ended in eagles' claw-and-ball feet.

Cabriole legs might still be hipped at the seat frame, and these wear-resisting corners might be carved with individual motifs or included in the all-over design covering also the brackets extending below the seat rail and the knees. Acanthus leaves and oak leaves have been noted. In one attractive design the knees were carved with lions' masks and the legs shaped to suggest hocks, with a wealth of feathery hair and paw feet. Front and back seat rails might extend downward, carved with expansive central motifs such as occasional satyrs' masks, or the more usual motifs matching the knee carving. Gilding might be applied to raised edges and carving. There was a vogue too for carved Red Indian masks on furniture: stools have been noted with this ornament in both mahogany and gilded softwood. Stools were also made in the gilded gesso fashionable during the first third of the eighteenth century, typical ornament consisting of a pattern of rosettes and strapwork in low relief on a pounced ground.

Chairs were already fashionable dining seats by early Georgian days and stools were no longer made in sets. A pair customarily matched a set of chairs. At the Stowe sale, 1848, Owen the antique dealer of New Bond Street paid £7 17s. 6d. for a pair of stools matching a set of six mahogany chairs carved with lions' heads, which were sold to another dealer for £28 7s. od. These were stated to have been made for the Duke of Chandos in the 1730s. A single mahogany stool with lion mask carving sold for sixty-five shillings.

Mahogany in the 1740s was expressing its individuality in a distinctive manner, but the demand for dining stools had ceased. Chippendale makes no mention of them in his *Director*, but Ince and Mayhew illustrate four stools in their *Universal System*, 1759–63, styling them "Lady's Dressing Stools". Two of these are X-framed with curved ends to their seats and the others have French legs, carved on the knees, with scroll and block feet. This drawing book also illustrates "French Stools for recesses of windows". That Chippendale made dressing stools is proved by his well-known bill to Sir Rowland Wynn, Nostell Priory, "2 dressing Stools Japan'd Green and Gold to match the [eight arm] Chairs and Stuff'd in Linnen £3.12s." These are still in existence, the stool legs matching the front legs of the chairs. Concave seats are a feature of dressing stools.

This period marked the decline of the cabriole leg in fashionable furniture. There was a return to square legs. These were straight, about 2 inches square and might be chamfered: another less frequent type was about 2½ inches wide and 1 inch thick. The front and side might be smoothly plain, or might be ornamented with lattice work either carved into the wood or introduced as an applied fret. Less frequently the legs were L-shaped in section, cut from the solid, and might be pierced and carved with trellis pattern and scrollwork. Such legs were often united by plain stretchers and ended in square feet. The seat rail might be decorated with a band of trellis-work or carved to suggest cut-card work. The leg-seat corners were filled with fret-cut angle brackets marrying with the design set in the seat rail.

When a cabriole leg design was used it was in a much lighter style, known at the time as a French leg, terminating in a scroll foot. The knee might be carved in relief with pendant acanthus leaves and scrolls, or flower sprays and fruit. Cluster column legs ending in small plinths were also used.

Double stools measuring from 4 to 6 feet in length became fashionable at this period and for the remainder of the century were placed against drawing-room walls, the wood panelling providing a warm back rest. Double stools had been used throughout the seventeenth century when they were known as banquet seats or banketts. The banquet was then a between-meal repast of fruit or sweetmeats served to guests. In the eighteenth century fruit and sweetmeats were served together as dessert, presented with lavish ostentation in the drawing-room shortly after dinner. Additional guests were often invited and might be seated on double stools when not standing or strolling about the room. Horace Walpole, writing in 1758, referred to such a banquet attended by the Prince of Wales and commented that "even on the stools were pyramids [glass stands filled with individual fruit and sweetmeat glasses] with troughs of strawberries and cherries".

The majority of drawing-room double stools were gilded or japanned. The six legs, cylindrical or square, tapered without interruption from seat rail to small moulded plinths, plain flutings emphasising their slenderness. Seat rails were linked by square blocks at the top of the legs and might have carved sunken panels, typically ornamented with pateræ.

In the deep window recesses were placed single stools with upward curved ends. Legs resembled those of double stools but seldom numbered more than four. The seat ends sloped outwards, rising for about a foot above the seat rail and ending with bold outward scrolls forming rests which were comfortably upholstered. The user could loll here to survey the outdoor scene. Later the rests were almost vertical. They were faced with flat rails carved or painted to match the seat rail which might be straight edged and narrow, less frequently curved on the lower edge. Caning might be used instead of upholstery.

Hepplewhite illustrates six window-seats in his *Guide*, 1788, recommending them as "peculiarly adapted for an

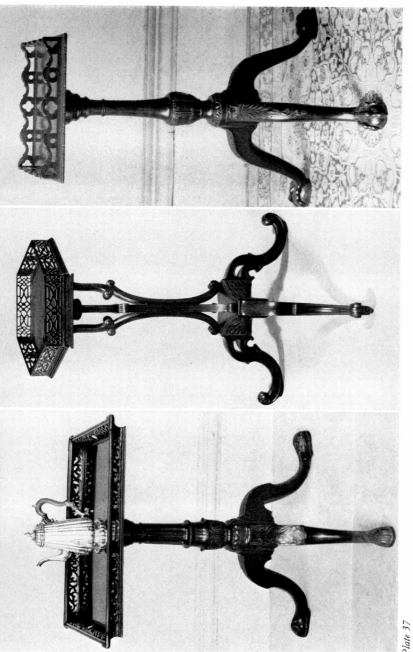

Plate 37

(*Left*) Mahogany tea-table with deep out-curving gallery carved and perforated, substantial fluted and carved pedestal and tripod with paw feet. (*Centre*) Tea-kettle or urn stand with fret-cut hexagonal gallery, open supporting shaft, and scrolled legs to the tripod. (*Right*) Tea-kettle or urn stand in carved mahogany with galleried top and claw-and-ball feet. 1760s.

Plate 38

(*Top left*) Mahogany tea-kettle stand with fretted gallery, baluster pillar, and feet with high insteps. (*Top right*) Early tea-urn stand in mahogany, its rectangular top surrounded by a fretwork gallery and its baluster stem carved with foliage and gadrooning. (*Lower left*) A tea-urn stand veneered in satinwood, mahogany and tulipwood, the oval top enriched with a shallow rim of ebony. Hepplewhite style. (*Lower right*) Tea-urn stand of carved mahogany with fretwork gallery of arcading and leafy scrolls; the frieze fitted with a sliding tray. The square legs have bevelled inner surfaces and cube feet.

elegant drawing-room of japanned furniture". The ends of all are scrolled. Some are set with open-work in the style of dining chairs, but even these have the upholstered scrolls. Others, however, were made with chair back ends and without the upholstered scrolls. Such stools were also made in satinwood and mahogany. A bill made out in 1790 by George Seddon, Sons & Shackleton entered these as French stools, charging £5 15s. 6d. in satinwood.

Hepplewhite's *Guide* also illustrates several designs for drawing-room stools, lighter and more delicately designed than any formerly made. He suggests that the round variety "is proper for a dressing stool" and that "the framework may be of mahogany or japanned, as most agreeable, or to match the suit of chairs, and of covering". He adds that the seats should not be higher than chairs. A typical example would be on moulded cabriole legs carved on the knees with anthemion medallions and rosettes terminating in French scroll feet. The ends might be either oval or rectangular.

Stools for the drawing-room remained in the Hepplewhite style until early in the nineteenth century. Then came a reversion to heavy-looking cumbersome styles in the Grecian and Egyptian taste, florid with ornament, and brilliant with paint, gilding and ormolu. *Ackermann's Repository*, published throughout the Regency years, illustrates a wide range of stools for use as "ornamental centre seats in elegant rooms". Some were of mahogany or rosewood, but soft woods were more usual, and from about 1818 might be bronzed. Others were ebonised. Frequently the legs swept outward in a concave curve: they displayed pateræ at seat level and might be reeded. There was also a bamboo style of leg with X-shaped stretchers, and the moulded cabriole legs continued to be made. Stools with X-frames or supports and scroll ends were fashionable, mostly attempting to follow classical designs.

Chapter Nineteen

TEA-CHESTS AND CADDIES

———

ENGLAND first tasted tea, somewhat timidly, in the early years of the Stewart kings, but not until the 1660s were its pleasures appreciated by the English hostess. The leaf was so costly that the mistress of the house guarded it under lock and key in tea-box, tea-trunk, tea-chest or tea-caddy. Here, for the first time, these treasure stores are differentiated.

The domestic stock of tea was originally kept in a tightly closed container. In 1675 Lord Rous's steward bought "a box of tin to keep his Lordship's tea in". This was not tinned iron plate as usually asserted, but a box made from plates of the finest quality moor tin, highly malleable and approaching the whiteness of silver in its lustre when burnished to close its grain. For formal use the tea was contained in wide-mouthed, short-necked, rectangular jars of red stoneware or blue and white porcelain from China. By the end of the century silver and pewter canisters had become fashionable, copying the shape of the Chinese jar.

The bulk tea was now kept in cube-shaped wooden tea-boxes lined with oriental tutenag foil and provided with lock and key to prevent petty pilfering. The account books kept in 1730 by Mrs. Knight, Dover Street, daughter of James Cragg, Secretary of State, record the prices paid for tea and a tea-box: 6 lb. finest Imperial tea cost 16s. lb.; 6 lb. Hyson tea 24s. lb.; tea-canister (pewter) 9d., mahogany tea-box 18s.

A pair of tea-canisters in silver, pewter, wood or japanned iron would be protected in a handsome leather-covered box with an arched lid shaped like a travelling trunk. These were known as tea-trunks and provided two qualities of tea for the hostess to blend at the tea-table where the luke-warm liquid was supped and the aroma inhaled with polite murmurs of pleasure.

Tea-trunks were covered with scarlet or green morocco leather, or the longer-wearing shagreen and enriched with silver lock mounts. By the 1740s the rims of box and cover were enclosed in silver, the visible surface engraved with intricate scrollwork. By the mid-eighteenth century the tea-trunk had given way before the flat-topped rectangular tea-chest which might be covered in shagreen. This was defined in Ash's *Dictionary*, 1775, as "a kind of small cabinet in which tea is brought to table".

Soon a central canister was introduced to contain sugar. Dean Swift provided confirmation of this in his *Directions to Servants*, 1745, noting "the invention of small trunks and chests, with lock and key wherein they keep the tea and sugar". The sugar-canister contained crushed sugar royal, the finest sugar then obtainable. This was trebly refined to remove the treacly flavour which hostesses had been wont to disguise by adding peach leaves to their tea.

The tea-chest also contained a silver mote skimmer. This was a spoon with a perforated bowl and a slender spear-topped stem, the latter used for clearing tea leaves from the teapot spout. The skimmer was used for removing the tea dust—known to Georgians as motes—floating on the surface of the liquid after it had been poured into the cup. These motes were caught on the silver surface of the skimmer.

The East India Company held the English tea monopoly until 1834, but in 1784 it was compelled by Government action to make drastic reductions in the prices of its teas. Tea still remained expensive but improved standards of living helped to increase consumption. Tea-pots were doubled in size and tea-canisters designed correspondingly larger. The demand for tea-chests increased as the price of tea lessened and few thrifty homes lacked a simple tea-box in mahogany or some less pretentious wood. Almost every branch of the furniture-making trade made tea-chests. Sixteen of the trade cards illustrated by Sir Ambrose Heal in his *London*

Furniture Makers and dating between 1749 and 1790 carry references to tea-chests, no other term being used. The engravings show several examples all, with one exception, large enough to accommodate three canisters or cube-shaped tea-boxes.

William Kirk, cabinet-maker "at the Sign of the Golden Chair, the Corner of Salisbury Street in ye Strand, London", 1749, illustrates a tea-chest with flat faces, a fixed D-handle on the flat top, and four scroll feet. Landall & Gordon "Joyners, Cabinet, & Chair-Makers at Ye Griffin & Chair in Little Argyle Street, by Swallow Street", about 1750, offer a lavishly carved tea-chest of bombé outline, a lid with receding sides and flat top, a carved keyhole escutcheon and four outward spreading paw feet. This closely resembles a tea-chest illustrated by Chippendale in his *Director*, 1762. John Potts, upholder, King Street, Covent Garden, about 1760, also shows a bombé tea-chest supported on four tall scrolled feet of cast metal—silver or ormolu. The matching keyhole escutcheon is heavily expansive and the flat top of the lid enriched with a cast handle extending from end to end with wide terminals.

Other trade cards, issued during the 1770s and 1780s, illustrate plain rectangular tea-chests with receding flat-topped lids, and with small scroll feet. Richard Holmes "at the Tea Chest in Barbican", 1785, is first to illustrate a tea-caddy. This is a hexagonal example with an expansive escutcheon and a large D-shaped hinged handle. The same card also announces "Tea Chests for Exportation".

Instead of metal canisters the majority of tea-chests during this period contained snugly fitting tea-boxes with hinged or sliding lids often bearing silver or ivory labels naming the tea, such as green or bohea. These boxes were locked beneath their hinged covers. They were lined with a metal foil made from an alloy known as tea-lead, a form of hard pewter. The lid of the tea-chest and its box compartments were lined with coloured velvet or flowered brocade edged with narrow braid.

Tea-boxes of mahogany now became ornamental and were used by those who preferred unblended teas on informal occasions: Chippendale's *Director*, 1762, illustrates

160

Plate 39
Tripod teapoys. (*Top left*) In satinwood with slender turned pillar and convex tripod. Late eighteenth century. (*Top right*) Mahogany with hexagonal stem and convex tripod. Late eighteenth century. (*Lower left*) Mahogany with open pillar and carved ornament. (*Lower right*) Mahogany with cluster-column stem and paw feet. Mid-eighteenth century.

11+

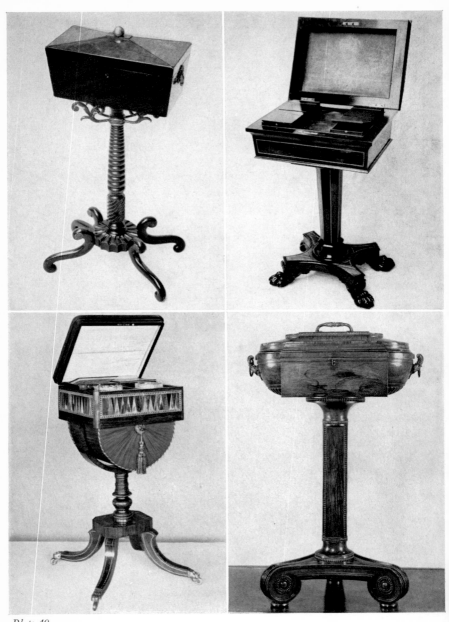

Plate 40
Teapoys. (*Top left*) Mahogany with turned pillar, scroll feet and ormolu bracket support beneath the tea-chest. (*Top right*) Inlaid with mother-of-pearl fitted with four tea-boxes and depressions for glass sugar and tea-blending bowls. (*Lower left*) Rosewood decorated with marquetry of various woods arranged in geometrical patterns. (*Lower right*) Regency teapoy in rosewood with ormolu fittings.

an oval example in carved mahogany, its width just about half that of a tea-chest. These eventually became known as caddies to distinguish them from tea-chests, from the Malayan weight *Kati*. The term caddy appears to have been used in the 1770s. Henry Clay, the celebrated Birmingham japanner, invoiced a "tea cade" to Horace Walpole in 1778. The earliest use of caddy given by the *Oxford English Dictionary* dates to 1792 when the *Madras Courier* of 2nd December reported "a Quantity of Tea in Quarter Chests and Caddies" and on the nineteenth of the following month Cowper wrote to Lady Hesketh, "When you went you took with you the key of the caddy". Eventually in the early nineteenth century the term tea-chest was outmoded in favour of tea-caddy. Thomas Sheraton in *The Cabinet Dictionary*, 1803, wrote that "the word caddy is now applied to the various kinds of tea chests".

Early tea-chests were made from solid mahogany con-structed by first-class cabinet-makers and lavishly carved with foliage, scrolls, shells, pendant husks and so on. Chippendale illustrates eight designs for tea-chests in his *Director*, all of them miniatures of the bombé commodes then fashionable. They are shown rectangular and in serpentine shape, on four scroll or rococo corner feet. Their width is rather less than a foot—suitable for three canisters or two cube-shaped boxes. In these designs the lid is hollow so that the canisters or boxes rise about an inch above the rim of the chest, just enough for them to be gripped back and front for withdrawal. The receding concave lid allows space for the finials ornamenting many canister lids.

Chippendale's tea-chests are decorated with heavily carved lock escutcheons either shaped in the solid wood or applied and with ormolu foliage handles on their tops. Alternatively, he recommends heavy mounts of ormolu. Existing examples dating from about 1760 show that expansive open-work mounts, saw-cut from substantial silver plate or in double-gilded brass plate, were becoming fashionable enrichments on mahogany tea-chests. These included escutcheons and corner brackets.

Less costly tea-chests also were made in solid mahogany. *The World*, No. 64, 1754, describes a tea-chest built and carved as a pile of bound books bearing leather labels inscribed with such a title as *Pope's Works*, placed alternately back and front, the lid, hinges and keyholes being cleverly concealed. There was a later vogue for a plainly rectangular tea-chest, its lid supporting a carved book with an inlaid upper cover acting as a lid to a small box containing a silver caddy ladle. Another series was designed with a small drawer set in one side of the base to receive a caddy spoon.

Lighter, more colourful tea-chests became fashionable from the early 1770s. Panels of veneered satinwood, harewood, burr walnut, cocoa wood and fruit woods were cleverly quartered to obtain natural grain effects. Carcases for the finer of such tea-chests were usually in red deal and this, with the veneer, required to be correctly seasoned to prevent unequal shrinkage and consequent cracking of the veneer. Inspection of the interiors of second-class and later tea-chests has shown that ends of wood were often used for carcase work, giving rise to the theory that tea-chest and caddy making was a spare-time occupation. It should be remembered in this connection that cabinet-makers worked from 6 a.m. to 8 p.m. on six days of the week.

Hepplewhite's *Guide*, 1788, reflecting the fashion of the previous decade or more, illustrates five examples, all elaborately inlaid with scrollwork and urns in all-over designs: two bombé shaped tea-chests and one rectangular; an oval caddy, and a square one. Four stand flat upon the tea-table and one has short bracket feet.

The corners of a tea-chest might be canted and decorated with vertical lines of stringing in contrasting colours between a pair of cross-banded columns. Each of the four faces of the chest might display an oval medallion in holly worked by the burnt sand process. Satinwood might be set with ovals of finely grained burr walnut and narrow bands of ebony.

Handles became less cumbrous and much reduced in size as the century progressed. Ornate ormolu was superseded by a plain D-shaped handle hinging at each end into a pair of collared sockets inserted into the lid and immovably fixed by means of thin square nuts and washers below. These were followed by the fixed upright loop handle, rising from a short collared stem. In others the loop was hinged from a flat plate of a shape following that of the chest outline.

The so-called Sheraton tea-chests continued to be veneered, satinwood and rosewood being favoured. Marquetry was less intricate than formerly although checker patterns might frame marquetry motifs in polychrome, or monochrome, such as medallions of shells, scrollwork, lozenges, wreaths, sprays of flowers and foliage, that were immediately associated with the decorative treatments of the day. In the 1790s they were trimmed with little brass ball feet matching the silver balls on teapots, and had brass ring handles. Solid keyhole escutcheons were featured, engraved with the owner's crest or monogram. The lid interior might be set with a panel of satinwood or other exotic wood in a colour contrasting with the exterior ground.

Tea-chests in mahogany still continued and from about 1790 were usually ornamented with stringing or variations of plaited inlay, the lids of the enclosed tea-boxes displaying matching ornament. There were also neat modifications of fluting suggestive of linen-fold carving together with fan, shield and urn-shaped ornaments. The keyhole escutcheon was frequently in ivory set in a diamond of ebony, or of ebony set within mother-of-pearl.

The pendulum of fashion swung backward in about 1810, re-introducing the commode shape of Chippendale's day but in heavy, clumsy versions of fine workmanship. Rosewood, dark mahogany, amboyna and maple were the woods most frequently preferred, inlaid with mother-of-pearl, brass or ebony. The lid interior was fitted with a bevelled mirror, or, less expensively, covered with lightly embossed papers in red or green.

Oval tea-caddies filled with tea made handsome gifts in the late eighteenth century. These were made "of these most curious English and Foreign Woods" enriched with colourful inlay in all-over designs. In red beech they were vividly painted with conventional flowers, encircling landscapes and allegorical scenes, festoons, medallions or coats of arms in full colours.

Octagonal caddies, that is rectangular with clipped

163

corners, date from the early 1770s onwards. These were usually enlivened with inlay or marquetry on each face. The front might display a shield in silver plate engraved with a crest, monogram or inscription. There was also a passing vogue for urn-shaped caddies on stemmed feet, resembling contemporary knife or fork cases.

Some attractive tea caddies were of sycamore, burr beech, and various fruit woods in forms resembling fruit such as melons, pears and apples, the upper portion opening as a lid. The melon-shaped caddy was divided into apparent segments by longitudinal inlay. Some later examples were fitted at the "stalk" with wide oval handgrips of silver. In the nineteenth century such caddies were made in boxwood and lignum vitae. The tea known as gunpowder was preserved in caddies resembling gunpowder flasks. This was a tea made from tender green leaves rolled individually so that each had a granular appearance somewhat resembling gunpowder. Tea-caddies were popular late Georgian gifts. Some were of red beech overlaid with plates of ivory, tortoiseshell or mother-of-pearl and others were of colourful papier-mâché.

Chapter Twenty

TEA-KETTLE AND URN-STANDS

TEA in Queen Anne's day was but a feeble counterpart of the fragrant amber liquid of today. The costly tea-leaves were imported from China in airtight vessels of tutenag (a pewter-like alloy), each dried leaf tightly rolled by hand, but the infusion was advertised in the *Tatler*, 1710, by R. Fary, at the Bell in Grace Church Street, London, as "of a light gray colour".

Tea-making instructions recorded by J. Worlidge in 1692 directed that a quart of clean water should be boiled "and then add a few dry leaves, which you may take up at once between the tips of your fingers, and let them thus stand in a covered Pot two or three minutes, in which time the leaves will be spread to their former breadth and shape and yield that bitter, yet pleasant taste. This Liquor you may, if you please, edulcorate with a little Sugar, and make it an acceptable Drink". The out-spread tea-leaves were removed from the pot to the voider by means of a silver straining spoon.

By this time it had become known that the water must be freshly boiling and it became customary for the hostess to prepare the tea herself in boudoir or drawing-room. This she did in a silver tea-pot supported by a handled tripod over a burning spirit lamp. The water was boiled in the tea-pot, the tiny rolled tea-leaves being added to the water immediately it came to the boil. Such equipage is shown by Thomas Hudson in his painting *John Gray and his family taking tea*.

It was soon noticed that the taste was improved if the boiling water were poured over the costly tea-leaves which were now put in the pot first. The pot was then half-filled

165

with boiling water, the leaves allowed to infuse for three minutes, and the pot then filled up with more boiling water.

A tea-kettle was first introduced to the silver tea equipage during the 1680s, taking its place over the spirit lamp. Kettle and lamp were not placed on the tea-table itself, however, but were mounted on a low tripod stand of wood or silver about 2 feet high. This stood upon the floor beside the tea-table. The delightful conversation piece *The Tea Party* in the National Gallery shows such a kettle-stand in use, the spirit lamp aflame, the boiling kettle held poised above the tea-pot by the tea-blender.

The Female Spectator of 1744 reported that a fashionable tea-table was more costly to maintain than two children and a nurse. A maid was appointed as tea-blender to superintend the tea-table and care for its equipage of precious silver and fragile porcelain; she also blended and served the tea. She prepared early morning tea for the family, served in the mistress's bedroom with full ceremony; then, following afternoon dinner and until candles were lit in the evening, she blended and served fresh tea to the unceasing flow of "Beaus and Women, Fans and Mechlin Lace" received in the drawing-room. Lady Hamilton in her younger days was employed as tea-blender to Sir Henry Fetherstonhaugh.

A tea-kettle stand in solid silver might be included in the fashionable Georgian tea-table equipage. Its baluster stem rising from a tripod might support a plate resembling a salver to hold the kettle and lamp, or perhaps the spirit lamp itself with three scroll brackets to hold the kettle ring.

More usually, however, kettle stands were modified versions of the pillar-and-claw or tripod table in walnut or heavy mahogany (see Chapter 16). The stem might be in baluster outline or consist of a fluted column rising from a bulb shape carved with gadrooning or acanthus leaves. Stem variants included the spirally fluted pillar and the more ambitious design formed of double or treble S-scrolls suggested flying buttresses. Many of the finest stands were vigorously carved throughout their length, the decoration continuing into the claws. Projecting from the base of the stem were the three claw legs in cabriole outline ending in ball-and-claw, pad, or lion's-paw feet. Claw variations of the mid-eighteenth century included the French dolphin form and scrolled and knurled toes. In well-designed examples the legs are so arched and poised that the feet appear to grip the floor.

The stem supported a top resembling a contemporary silver salver, its diameter approximating that of the tea-kettle body. A simple top might be plainly circular or shaped in a series of deep scallops, the surface sunk a little below a shapely carved moulding resembling the edge of a silver tray. Such a top was carved from the solid plank of wood, never joined, and this was true, too, of the more elaborate "pie-crust" designs in which the raised and moulded edge was shaped in a series of sharp curves and points.

Soon after the mid-century the top of a fashionable tea-kettle stand was encircled by a gallery. This might be solid, fretted, or constructed of a series of turned spindles, and was intended to prevent the kettle and its boiling contents from falling when the floor vibrated. Chippendale illustrates such a tea-kettle stand on Plate LV of *The Gentleman and Cabinet-Maker's Director*, 1762. This has a scalloped top encircled by a wavy-edged gallery pierced with upright ovals. The scrolled feet are supported on solid horizontal bases to increase stability. A somewhat similar tea-kettle stand with a curved stem of fine baluster outline and scroll feet is illustrated by Ince and Mayhew in their *Universal System*, 1759–62. The stem carving and gallery fretwork are designed to match. Such stands were not fitted with the snap hinges that enabled the tops of pillar-and-claw tables to be tipped up and placed against the wall when not in use. A tea-kettle stand when not in use was slipped beneath the tea-table, the two pieces of furniture often having matching galleries and other motifs.

Although silver tea-kettles continued in use they were outmoded for more than half a century by the tea-fountain which came into use in about 1760, followed by the tea-urn. The tea-fountain was the first step towards the urn: the kettle was modified by replacing the spout with a ball-handled tap inserted close to the broad base. This rather ugly vessel and its lamp then stood on the tea-kettle stand.

This unshapely design was quickly altered, however,

acquiring the urn form of the vessels then fashionable in blue-john and pottery, with narrow neck, wide-topped tapering body, short pedestal stem rising from a square plinth, and, at first, moulded handles attached to the shoulders. The body of such an urn, which was charcoal-heated, contained no more than a quart of water.

Charcoal-heated tea urns began to be superseded from 1774 by those in which an iron was used to heat the water. This cast-iron cylinder, made red hot in the kitchen fire, was inserted into a close-fitting heater-case or deep socket rising centrally from the base within the urn so that the water circulated around it. Ten years later Cowper noted "the bubbling and loud-hissing urn throwing up a steamy column". This innovation was patented by John Wadham, a brazier of St. George-in-the-East, London. The patent specification No. 1076 is accompanied by a sketch illustrating a sectional view of such an urn. The patentee is known to have supplied copper heating cases and box-irons to the Sheffield platers at five shillings each.

Soon it was realised that the tea-urn tap was to be an unending source of trouble to both users and makers, whether in silver, Sheffield plate or copper. The soft metal from which the taps were made rendered them liable to drip slowly soon after being taken into regular use: also they were easily bent. Difficulty was experienced, too, in fitting the tap firmly with its strengthening plates inside and outside the container. Under careless usage leaks quickly developed. Not until the 1820s was the urn-tap made foolproof by casting in a single piece.

At first the tea-urn stood upon the kettle-stand with a galleried rectangular top, its narrow end facing the user. The urn was placed towards the back of the stand so that its tap could project over a small silver or porcelain drip basin. This was pushed aside to permit insertion of the small tea-pots then in vogue. As urns became more capacious a full vessel complete with its box-iron was exceedingly heavy and the tripod stand no longer provided adequate stability.

Both Chippendale and Ince & Mayhew illustrate tea-kettle stands in the form of a metal-lined box mounted on four cabriole legs. Chippendale noted that these "are so easy to understand that they want no explanation". It has not been realised, however, by present-day collectors that such stands were intended to hold the early tea-fountains and charcoal-heated tea-urns as protection against accidental overturning. A slot was cut to accommodate the projecting tap, and a slide for the tea-pot to rest on was fitted beneath.

These cumbersome articles achieved little measure of popularity and were quickly superseded by the urn-stand with four out-splayed legs supporting a square top. Such a piece might be made *en suite* with its accompanying tea-table. Inserted in the underframe, immediately below the table top, was a sliding shelf, extending almost to the rear edge when pushed back out of use. When drawn out it held the tea-pot being filled with boiling water, and at other times a small drip bowl. The surface of the slide was given a shallow circular or oval depression to prevent bowl or tea-pot from slipping off. At first the slide measured about 4 inches in width; during the late 1770s it was increased to about 6 inches; by the end of the century it might run to the full width of the frieze.

It is frequently stated that the tea itself was made in eighteenth-century urns and drawn off into the tea-cups placed upon the slide. Several conversation pieces of the period contradict this theory, however, including James Northcote's painting of 1783, "Doctor Johnson Taking Tea with Sir Joshua Reynolds and his Niece, Miss Theophila Palmer". Miss Palmer is depicted in the act of filling a porcelain tea-pot from a bell-shaped tea-urn. Again, in 1797, *Prices of Cabinet Work* describes urn-stands as being fitted "with a slider for the tea-pot to stand on". There is no clear evidence that tea for drinking in the home was made directly in the urn.

Early four-legged urn-stands were galleried and of sturdy construction in mahogany. Johann Zoffany's conversation piece "The 14th Lord Willoughby de Broke and his Family" illustrates a tall silver tea-urn of Adam design standing upon a four-legged urn-stand with stretchers, its square top encircled by a gallery of turned spindles fitting the square plinth of the urn. Both urn and stand are still in possession of the family.

In the Victoria and Albert Museum is a mahogany urn-stand with a fretwork gallery of arcading and leafy scrolls, the frieze fitted with a slide. The four square legs are without stretchers. They are bevelled on the inner surfaces and have cube feet. The top measures 10½ inches square and its height is 23¼ inches. There are angle brackets of fretwork. Frets used for gallery work were strong by reason of their construction—three layers of wood glued together in different ways of the grain. There were many variants of this design. The top was often serpentine in outline, and the gallery fretwork design in a well-made piece might be repeated in low relief carving on the legs and in pierced work on diagonal stretchers; yet other legs were in the scrolling cabriole outline.

Fashion now called for more colourful woods than the conventional mahogany. These included satinwood, popular in both solid and veneer between 1770 and 1795, harewood (stained sycamore), tulip, rosewood and kingwood, all usually enriched with inlay or marquetry in contrasting colours. The urn-stand top might display a panel of beautifully figured wood or might be set with attractive marquetry work. The frieze was frequently fluted, carved with *pateræ* at the corners, and accompanied by fluted legs. Plain stretchers intersecting at the centre were usual and continued throughout the period. One alternative design consisted of four diagonal stretchers with uprising curves dove-tailed into a central urn-shaped bulb.

By the time Hepplewhite's *Cabinet Maker and Upholster's Guide* was published in 1788, urn tables were already more delicately designed in colourful woods. The *Guide* illustrates five patterns for urn-stands, all their tops designed for tea-urns with square plinths. They are square, square with bowed sides, octagonal and round, their galleries either pierced or solid, with a wavy edge. All are fitted with tea-pot slides. Stretchers no longer connect the slender splayed legs. Hepplewhite notes that urn stands "may be inlaid of various woods or painted and varnished", and recommends a height of about 26 inches.

From about 1790 tea-urns might be heated with spirit lamps, the flat-based water container, resembling an Indian funerary urn in form, being supported by four flat columns rising from a flat rectangular plinth bearing the spirit lamp. The tops of stands intended for such urns were rectangular, oval, or in serpentine outline. Satinwood was popular at this period, painted with festoons and medallions. Japanned urn-stands were made, too, and were described by Sheraton as for "inferior drawing rooms". These, it must be assumed, were intended to support tea-urns of Pontypool or Birmingham japanned iron ware in glowing hues of crimson, blue and green, enriched with gilding.

By 1800 there was a fashionable reversion from four-legged urn-stands to the tripod. The urn-stand was defined in George Smith's *Household Furniture*, 1808, as a "tray-top supported by a central pedestal 2½ feet high, on tripod feet to stand beside the tripod tea-table which it matches in mahogany, and holds the tea urn". This suggests that the early nineteenth-century pedestal stands were intended for urns. These had slender concave or convex claw legs raised on long pointed feet. Often there was a small pointed pendant finial below the pillar, which was plain and well-turned. Carving has been added sometimes to late mahogany tripod urn-stands in an effort to enhance their value under the term of kettle-stand.

The old tea-table ritual declined and eventually vanished during the Napoleonic wars, the tea-urn taking a dominating place upon the tea-tray, as it had done in less pretentious homes from the 1770s.

Chapter Twenty-one

T HE Georgian architect commissioned to plan a new country mansion included in his design a stone-built temple raised on an eminence or set against a background of magnificent trees and facing lawns or water. These tall-windowed temples, with their doors opening on to stone terraces where musicians could play, were used during summer months for entertaining guests with light, between-meal repasts, and especially for partaking of tea. Behind the parlour furnished in rustic style was a small compartment where refreshments were prepared.

When the occasion called for tea this was made and served in the parlour by the tea-blender, usually the most attractive-looking girl among the household staff. The Duchess of Northumberland in her *Diary* for 1773 refers to an assembly where the tea blenders were "dressed in Jesuits Uniform of White Lustring with Blue Ribbons, & their heads were all very prettily dressed and exactly the same".

Whilst staying at Goodwood in 1781 Sylas Neville noted that "the Park has some pretty situations, particularly Kearny Seat, a tea-drinking place build on an eminence by the late Duke". Many lesser establishments at that time possessed similar fashionable garden retreats: in towns they might be raised on high stone columns to extend the view.

Each guest was served with tea on a small individual table supported by three splay legs and known as a teapoy, a word defined by the *New Oxford Dictionary* as "a small three-legged table especially for tea: from the Hindu *tin*, three, and the Persian *pae*, foot. The sense and the spelling influenced by tea".

Claw tables of finer craftsmanship were used for tea-drinking occasions in the house itself. These also were known as teapoys to distinguish them from the special tea-table where the hostess herself sat to serve tea on informal occasions. Elizabeth Hamilton, the well-known writer, when staying at Bulstrode with the Duke and Duchess of Portland and Mrs. Delany, wrote in her *Diary* that they "drank tea at seven, the Groom of the Chamber coming to say that it was ready. We each had our little table". Mrs. Delany herself, when visiting Queen Charlotte at Windsor Castle, noticed "the little tables from which we drank our tea".

The Duchess of Northumberland after a two-year absence on the Continent, observed a change in the royal service of 7 o'clock tea at St. James's Palace. She wrote in her *Diary* on 26th December 1772, "formerly the Queen made Tea herself at the Table and the King carried it about to the Ladies. Now, two Pages of the Backstairs enter'd each with a waiter carrying a single cup of Tea with Cream Pot and Sugar. One was given to each of their Majesties (on their teapoys) and then the Pages made their appearance again with Tea upon waiters for Lady Holdernesse and myself."

These claw-footed teapoys for the reception of individual cups, saucers and plates, measured about 30 inches in height, the pillars supporting octagonal tops about 15 inches across. Such tables date from early Georgian days, when they were made in sterling silver for supporting silver tea-kettles and their spirit lamps.

Claw teapoys made by the cabinet-makers and turners from fine woods may be traced throughout the reigns of George II and George III (1727–1820) in walnut, mahogany and satinwood, with pillars and claws following the changing styles of other tripod tables. By the 1780s the pillar had become more daintily slender than formerly, rising from three correspondingly slender claw legs in convex or concave curves extending the same distance as the table top and terminating in spade or plain feet. The three leg-pillar joints might be strengthened underneath by a bracket attachment cut from steel or latten plate and screwed into position. Latten was not ordinary brass, as generally supposed, but a tough-textured plate hammered from the ingot by the battery process. From about the middle of the eighteenth century the rim of the octagonal top was finished squarely and no longer shaped. Such a teapoy was light in weight, permitting it to be lifted with one hand.

Despite the royal lead, hostesses in less magnificent circumstances were unable to follow. The hostess continued making tea at her table, the host handing the cups: the use of individual teapoys declined. At this time the tea warehouses were crammed with unsaleable stocks, the result of widespread smuggling to avoid tax. The Duchess of Northumberland noted that the East India Company warehouses contained 2,500,000 lb. of tea, "yet all the common Retailers are so fully supplied that there is no Room for any sales that way".

As described in chapter nineteen, tea prices fell somewhat after 1784 and demand increased so that canisters or tea-boxes in their velvet-lined tea-chests were made larger than formerly. This style of tea-chest became known as a caddy in the 1790s. It was considerably larger and heavier than the shagreen-covered tea-chest that formerly had been part of the tea equipage and had rested on the carpet near to the hostess, as depicted in various conversation pieces such as "The Walpole Family" in the National Gallery, and "The Strode Family" in the Tate Gallery. The new caddy, therefore, found its place on a teapoy placed near to the hostess's tea-table which it matched in mahogany or other wood. Thomas Hope in *Household Furniture*, 1807, illustrated two examples of teapoys and noted that they stood beside the tea-table for the reception of the tea-caddy.

The caddy standing loosely upon the teapoy was in danger of being dislodged accidentally, and after about 1810 it was fixed instead directly to the pedestal, and the octagonal table top was discarded. The article of furniture thus developed retained the name teapoy, a term defined in Simmonds' *Dictionary of Trade*, 1850, as "an ornamental pedestal table with lifting top, for holding tea".

Until well into Queen Victoria's reign no fashionable tea equipage was considered complete without such a teapoy. At first the vertical pillar and three claw feet remained legacies from teapoys of the table type. But the slender stem and feet proved unsuitable supports for the unwieldy caddy. The vertical pillar was then made stronger, turned from the solid wood and rising from the solid rectangular block that held the four outspreading concave legs mounted on paw castors. By 1820 designers endeavoured, without much success, to give some teapoys a rococo appearance in harmony with the times. Thus a teapoy might have a turned pillar rising from a decorative plinth, often circular, supported by four scroll feet, the sides of the upper scrolls fitted with large brass rosettes. This brass work would harmonise with ornamental brass bracket supports extending horizontally from the pillar beneath the caddy.

Until about 1820 teapoy caddies were rectangular, of tapering sarcophagus shape, usually of mahogany, plain or inlaid with buhl or mother-of-pearl, less frequently of rosewood veneer with heavy brass side rings and lid finials. The caddy became considerably more capacious from about 1820 and was usually about 18 inches square, containing four rectangular compartments with hinged lids. These were separated, two on each side, by a pair of central openings containing cut-glass bowls each elaborately worked with a different design in deep relief. The rear bowl contained lumps of sugar nipped from the cone: in the front bowl the hostess blended her teas in the presence of her guests or family. In many instances the four rectangular compartments were fitted with loose tea-boxes sliding in so closely and smoothly that they could be lifted out with the slightest effort. There might be provision, too, for sugar tongs and one or two caddy ladles, all in silver. Lids were lined with coloured velvet or plush.

The personal blending of teas was customary owing to the risk of adulteration to shop-blended teas by the tea-grocers, of whom there were more than thirty thousand, in addition to the china-sellers who also stocked full ranges of teas. If preparations known as smouch were added to blended teas they were difficult to detect, although visible at a glance in unblended teas. Country people found the preparation of smouch a profitable pin-money occupation during the summer months: for black tea smouch consisted of dried ash leaves; for green tea, dried elder buds. Hence the frequent personal selection of unblended tea from the tea-man's chest for home-blending in the teapoy.

The heavy caddy naturally required the support of a sturdier pillar than formerly, octagonal on plan and either in inverted baluster shape or a straight column. Such a pillar rose from the centre of a heavy, expansive cross-shaped plinth, the angles between the arms rounded, their terminals carved into the shape of four massive paw feet with castors beneath. When the caddy was inlaid, the upper surface of the plinth was decorated with matching inlay. The lid opened on a pair of strong brass hinges designed to hold it firmly a little beyond the vertical. The lid interior might be of polished wood: later bevelled mirrors of high quality plate glass were fitted.

Teapoys of papier-mâché had a fashionable vogue for more than half a century. They were highly colourful and had the additional advantage of being much lighter in weight than those of wood which they eventually superseded. Burrell and Yule writing in 1886 noted them on display at the London japan ware shops at that time. The earliest and finest were of paper-ware, consisting of sheets of specially prepared paper pasted one upon the other over shaped moulds and then japanned. Less costly teapoys in papier-mâché date from the early 1840s, constructed by cabinet-makers from shaped units made from rag pulp pressed into thick blocks. Details regarding papier-mâché appear in Chapter 15.

Pillars in both types were plain round balusters rising from rectangular plinths with incurved sides and clipped corners mounted on paw or turned feet with castors. In pulp-made examples the bulge of the baluster is far more pronounced than was formerly the case. Papier-mâché teapoys made before the mid-1830s were decorated over coloured grounds: afterwards the japan grounds were almost invariably black.

The papier-mâché teapoy lid, always a field for attractive ornament, was hinged the full width of the caddy and protected from strain when open by chains or automatic clip devices. The top surface was often decorated with an

Plate 41

Swivel toilet glasses. (*Top left*) Veneered with short strips of cross-grained walnut. (*Top right*) Mahogany, fitted with crest and stretcher, on a stand containing three drawers with concave shaping. Mid-eighteenth century. (*Lower left*) Oval mirror on serpentine stand with ogee feet, the mahogany veneer bordered with stringing. 1780s. (*Lower right*) Japanned bureau type on a stand with cross stretchers. The desk front opens on to small bearers and there is a candlestick slide at the side.

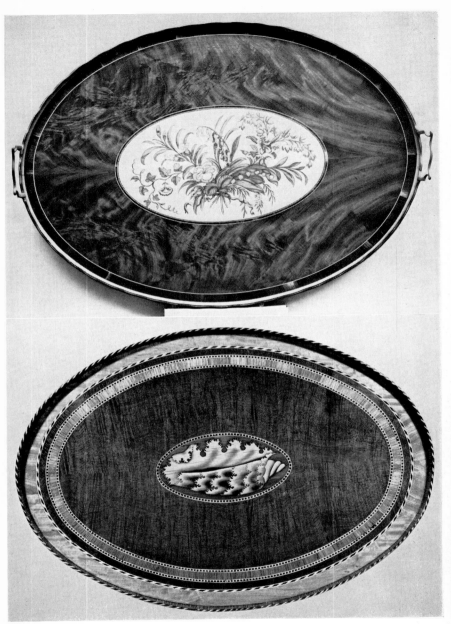

Plate 42
Oval trays. (*Top*) Decorated with sycamore, holly, partly stained, and kingwood. The marquetry central panel contains a bouquet of carnations, hyacinths and other flowers. The edge of the rim has a wavy outline. Brass handles. (*Below*) With stringing ornament to the borders of satinwood, mahogany and kingwood, and a central shell motif of sand-burnt holly. 1790s.

oil painting, such as a country view, or an animal study, or less ambitious flowers and foliage. Others were set with mother-of-pearl tinted with transparent paint. The rarest today are those set with foil-backed gems.

The name teapoy is sometimes wrongly used to designate the porcelain or pottery vessel termed a tea-jar in such contemporaneous evidence as the Worcester sale catalogue of 1769, and the catalogue of the Great Exhibition of 1851.

Chapter Twenty-two

TOILET GLASSES

THE fashionable beauty in Charles II's London enhanced her charms at a toilet table lavishly draped and bearing a brilliant array of silver toilet accessories. These included unguent boxes, essence pots, silver-handled brushes, a pair of candlesticks, and, most important, a silver-framed mirror often with an engraved detachable cresting. This stood against a draped background, its slope adjusted by a hinged strut screwed to the backboard.

If she could afford such luxury she hung a wall mirror immediately above dressing-table level, aggrandised by a wide frame of walnut or japanned wood. Its thin, almost square, plate might be finished with blunt-edged bevels, but more usually was plain. The frame was in a convex section bead or simple ogee moulding. In walnut this was built from short lengths of cross-grained veneer laid over a deal foundation; japanning was applied on solid beechwood. A gilt fillet between glass and frame gave additional elegance and a solid cresting was usual. By the end of the century the top of the frame might be arched or curved and the cresting abandoned.

Dressing-mirrors of this type, for standing on the dressing-table or hanging above it, continued to be made throughout the eighteenth century. Lady Grisell Baillie in 1715 paid £2 14s. 0d. for "2 walnut dressing Glasses for my self and Grisie with drawers". In mahogany with panelled backboards they cost about a guinea each during the 1750s. John Hodson, an eminent looking-glass and cabinet-maker of Frith Street, London, illustrated a dressing-glass on his trade card of the 1730s. The sketch shows a marble-topped dressing-table

178

with a strut-back mirror in a walnut ovolo frame. This has straight sides and lower edge with a shaped top. The card records that these were in the "most Fashionable manner, made by choice and experienc'd Workmen employ'd in his own house".

The dressing-table and looking-glass were developed as independent units until the mid-eighteenth century. In the first years of the century the mirror was particularly attractive with its arched top, its bevelled glass, and a gilded fillet which might have a wavy edge. But it was transformed into a distinctive piece of furniture when cabinet-makers introduced the Dutch idea of mounting it on uprights by means of a screw-action movement which enabled it to be tilted to any angle and held there.

These fitments attached the mirror to a pair of slender uprights at a point slightly above half their height. The uprights, raking slightly backward, were either straight-sided, turned or fluted, and were topped by ornamental finials, often in ivory. Such a mirror was usually solid-crested with a wavy outline, the uprights terminating in line with the lower end of the arch.

The uprights obviously required a solid base and for this purpose nests of drawers and miniature bureaux were designed and fitted to contain toilet requisites. Such a unit might be in deal veneered with walnut or, more expensively, with burr walnut, to match the mirror frame. Most usually the base was built up in three receding tiers of drawers, the lowest consisting of one long drawer, the other tiers with up to seven small drawers, their minute pulls being in gilded silver or brass. Drawer fronts were usually shaped in concave curves, both vertically and horizontally. Drawer interiors were neatly constructed with mortice and tenon joints in thin oak, black walnut and eventually in mahogany. Four small feet raised the piece about an inch above the dressing-table. Bracket feet were general and might be set beneath splayed corners, with or without a very shallow plinth. Turned feet were also used.

In many instances the upper drawers were concealed, and the contents protected from pilfering servants, beneath a slanting fall-front which usually opened on to a pair of pull-out side bearers. This space was meticulously fitted with movable pilasters, pigeon-holes, a central cupboard, and ivory-knobbed drawers, designed exactly as in full-size writing bureaux. Below was a single drawer extending the full width of the piece, averaging about 18 inches. This was fitted with divisions for canisters, covered boxes, and a pin cushion stuffed with emery powder. Examples exist complete with their original japanned containers for toilet requisites. In a few instances the drawer was provided with semi-cylindrical ends corbelled out to support the flap instead of bearers. Arrow pattern bands of inlay or marquetry might ornament plain surfaces. The keyholes on the fall-front and lower drawer possessed expansive silver or gilded brass escutcheons with wavy rims.

Red or black japanned dressing-glasses, decorated with Chinese figures and flower sprays in gold and colours, were fashionable until the 1730s. All-over tortoiseshell veneer introduced even more richly glowing colour to luxury specimens between about 1715 and 1730. These had ornamental mounts and corner pieces of pierced silver plate, and silver feet.

Until the early 1730s a dressing-glass, whether japanned or in walnut, might fit snugly on a table-high matching stand. Early examples had four square legs with cross-stretchers: later they were L-shaped without stretchers. But the whole design of the bureau dressing-glass was eventually outmoded as the dressing-table with fitted drawers was evolved. Upon this, from the mid-1730s, stood a less costly dressing-glass in walnut, its rectangular mirror mounted on nothing more elaborate than a double tier of drawers daintily shaped in various serpentine outlines.

Mirror glass of the eighteenth century had a watery appearance with a slightly grey tinge. Preparation of the transparent plate into the mirror recognised by collectors was carried out by a process not yet duplicated on reproductions. The glass was delivered in the rough to mirror-makers where it was fixed to a horizontal table and above it placed a smaller plate supporting a box weighted with stones. Fine sand and water were sprinkled over the lower plate and the upper was worked over it in all directions. In

Plate 43
Oval trays. (*Top*) Mahogany inset with satinwood and kingwood, with brass handles. About 1770. (*Centre*) Mahogany with pierced gallery and carved hand-holds. About 1760. (*Bottom*) Butler's tray of coopered mahogany bound with brass. 1770s.

Plate 44

(*Top left and centre*) Two views of a mahogany cellaret with two service slides and writing-desk. About 1800. (*Top right*) Brass-bound _____ cellaret on stand in the Chippendale style. (*Lower left*) Oval wine cistern in mahogany, made in sections on carved stand this way each planed the other's surface. When the surfaces of both glasses had become perfectly flat they were smoothed by introducing finer sand and finally finished with powdered emery.

The plate was then embedded in plaster of paris which held it firmly whilst its surface was polished. A flexible rod known as a bow was bent and one end fixed to the ceiling, the lower end of a polishing block lined on the underside with a coarse blanket. This was worked about over the glass. First it was charged with flour emery to remove scratches and blotches, then with tripoli to clear the ground, and its final lustre was achieved with putty powder. Both sides of the glass were so treated.

One side of the polished plate was then silvered. A sheet of thin blotting paper was spread upon a table and sprinkled with fine chalk. A sheet of tin foil was laid over this. Mercury was poured upon the foil and distributed over its entire surface with a hare's foot. Over the tin foil was laid a sheet of clean paper and over that the glass plate. With his left hand the worker pressed down the glass plate whilst his right hand gently withdrew the paper. The plate was then covered with thick paper and loaded with a weight so that superfluous mercury was pressed out, and the foil made to adhere closely to the glass. When dry the looking-glass was complete. This process was fully described in technical works of the early eighteenth century and again in *The Plate Glass Book*, 1777 edition, and it continued until the 1840s when a process was invented using pure silver.

Mahogany bedroom furniture was becoming fashionable by the 1740s, including a fitted dressing-table. The dressing-glass, now with a wide flat bevel, was rectangular and framed in narrow moulding, sometimes with a gilt fillet or with the inner edges gilded over carving in repeat motifs or wave ornament. Many, still, were framed in walnut. The frame's only shaping consisted of inward pointing corners at the top. In some instances a flat, fret-cut cresting is found as on contemporary mahogany wall mirrors. Uprights to support the glass, square, tapering and surmounted by tall turned mahogany finials, were mounted on the flat surface of a shallow box. This was in veneered pine, with small ovolo ornament encircling the top edge, and contained a single row of drawers, usually three, with concavely shaped faces. It was supported on a shallow plinth with short bracket feet: the plinth was rare after about 1750. In some instances, from the mid-1750s, a wide fret-cut stretcher was placed between the feet of the uprights.

Dressing-glasses from the late 1760s took on a variety of shapes derived from the shields and ellipses of chair backs and other curving forms. The mirror frame, narrow and with flat surfaces, was of cross-banded veneer upon a base constructed from short sections of pine. Rounded shapes were veneered on pliant wood such as yew. In the last quarter of the century many glasses were veneered in satinwood: other were japanned or painted.

Uprights obviously had to be gracefully curved and fitted closely against the mirror outline, rising from short vertical supports. These flat-sided uprights were tapered and on a shield-shaped mirror they extended to the lower point of the arch; on an oval mirror their inward curve was carried considerably beyond the screw mount. Scroll finials at top and bottom were enriched with carved bosses in ivory or contrasting wood. Cresting was not entirely abandoned: it is found variously in the form of fret-cut ornament, open-work carvings and solid crests inlaid or worked in marquetry with colourful flower ornament or painted with classical motifs.

The veneered box in bow or serpentine form with vertical rather than concave front, was fitted with three drawers, the central one with a lock, flanked by two of half its width. Their drop-loop handles were in either brass or silver, and the diamond-shaped keyhole escutcheon in ivory, like the three turned urn-shaped finials that often ornamented the arch of a shield-shaped glass. Lines and borders might be inlaid in contrasting woods such as satinwood, rosewood or

---

TOILET GLASSES

1. Marquetry ornamenting the broad ovolo mould and flat cresting; wide bevelled plate glass. 1690s. 2. Embroidery—raised or "stump" work—framed in tortoiseshell. Mid seventeenth century. 3. Silver; end of seventeenth century. 4. Walnut veneer, the fall-front opening on to pull-out rests. 5. Walnut veneer with flat cresting and shaped stretcher. About 1730. 6. Walnut veneer. 7. Walnut with deeply moulded frame and reeded pillars. 8. Mahogany, with fret-cut cresting and carving on the canted corners of the stand. 1760s. 9, 10. Mahogany often banded with satinwood. Late eighteenth century. 11. Mahogany with ivory finials and feet. Around 1800. 12. Early nineteenth century.

THEALE HUGHES

Fig. 6. Toilet Glasses

ebony, or in a small checker pattern in bone and ebony. By the 1770s the drawer fronts might be enriched with more elaborate colourful marquetry, such as swags of husks stained green, vari-coloured flowers and foliage, urns or medallions. The upper surface of the stand might be enriched with fanned marquetry pateræ, but was usually plain. Ogee bracket feet were usual.

Sheraton described fashionable dressing-glasses in his *Drawing Book*, 1791–3. He wrote: "some are fixed to a box containing three drawers about 3 inches deep, standing either upon small brackets or knobs for feet. The size of these dressing boxes runs from 22 to 28 inches in length and when they are serpentine they are from 10 to 12 inches in width."

Design was simplified by 1800 through the influence of the factory furniture makers to whom straight lines meant lower costs. The box and mirror were usually rectangular and all edges squared off with plain, flat faces which might be banded with satinwood or an inlay rope pattern. The mirror frame might be given a low, solid crest with a curved top. The supports were turned columns terminating in line with the top of the mirror frame and fitted with turned finials of ivory or bone, matched by a finial centred on the cresting. Drawers were fitted with expansive ivory or bone knobs and there was an inlaid diamond-shaped keyhole escutcheon, often in mother-of-pearl. Most usually turned knobs controlled the mirror movement.

So far the uprights had been placed near the back corners of the stand, their bases square in section. From about 1800 the turned uprights were fitted into triangular plinths pegged into the stand. The flat fronts of the plinths were almost vertical, in line with the mirror supports, and their edges were plain or reeded. By 1815 the turned supports rose high above the mirror-frame, and ring turnery might ornament the front corners of the box, sometimes bow-shaped and inlaid with brass lines. The mirror frame might have a convex surface and each drawer front was edged with a raised rim.

The bombé front had appeared by 1820 with two knob-less drawers and four scroll feet. The mirror swung between

Plate 45

Cellarets in mahogany. (*Top left*) Brass bound with domed lid and vase finial on low octagonal table with French style legs. (*Top centre*) Octagonal with flat lid and square tapered legs. (*Top right*) Brass bound octagonal with flat lid inlaid on top, and with stretchers to the inlaid square taper legs. (*Lower left*) Octagonal with enclosed storage space; on bracket feet. About 1800. (*Lower centre*) Octagonal on splay legs inlaid with lines. Early nineteenth century. (*Lower right*) Wine cistern with rectangular body and canted corners, on cabriole legs and paw feet. 1760s.

Plate 46

Work-tables. (*Top left*) Brass-inlaid rosewood with adjustable writing-board, brass gallery, slide inlaid as a chessboard, and pleated pouch. Early nineteenth century. (*Top right*) With satin-wood top over pleated pouch supported by a mahogany pedestal on four convex feet. (*Lower left*) In satinwood with mahogany stringing lines, fitted with fire-screen, adjustable top, writing-drawer and slide-out pouch. 1790s. (*Lower right*) Mahogany with satinwood stringing. The box is divided into compartments and the spindled shelf is for wool.

solid trestle posts, their feet extending from the front to the back of the box top and their front and back edges reeded. In these posts the lower half was cut from the flat wood, tapering, and was fitted with a turned upper portion. The mirror was square with a narrow moulded frame.

Chapter Twenty-three

AMONG the smaller creations of Georgian cabinet-makers trays are outstandingly decorative, their history long and their role of no small importance in the vast majority of homes where silver of such magnitude would have been unthinkable. Although long dominated by a minority of silver trays, they may be shown to have developed a range of distinct and delightful individualities, the word tray in this connection being used to include the voiders, tea-boards and hand-boards, as well as the trays of Georgian definition, to be considered in this survey.

Throughout their early history these articles were as ill-defined in their name as in their purposes. In general the term voider appears to have been used but this is now usually associated with the shallow rectangular tray specifically intended for clearing the waste food fragments during a meal, scraped from trencher and table with a voiding knife. Hence the word's appropriation for the receptacle used for clearing away not only food scraps but the piles of used plates. When the Georgian voiding pail for plates came into fashion for this duty, as a handsome vessel in brass-bound mahogany, it might be accompanied and matched by a voider for food fragments defined unpretentiously as "a pail-like article of wood or wicker into which bones are thrown during a meal".

Such specialised use of the term has now obscured its more general application in an early Georgian context. Bailey's dictionary, 1730, defined a voider as "a table basket for plates, knives, etc., also a painted or Japanned Vessel to hold Services of Sweetmeats". Yet even this application of the term had been used for centuries. At the coronation banquet of Edward VI in 1547 it was recorded that the sweetmeats were brought in arrayed on "a goodly voyde". It may be assumed that some sweetmeat voiders were then of silver but many more of wood. Examples are mentioned occasionally in Elizabethan inventories, and the *Lismore Papers* for 1630 record that Sir Richard Boyle sent an "old silver voyder to be exchanged for a new"—indication of a change in fashionable form such as would only be expected of an article in plentiful use.

In early Georgian days when dessert was served in a room apart from the main meal, voiders of japanned or painted wood introduced bold splashes of colour to set off the dainty fare. These were set out with individual glasses of whipped syllabubs, jellies, ice creams, lemon cream and so on, four or more voiders around the sides and ends of each table, flanked by dishes of fruit and dry sweetmeats. When the sweetmeat glasses were emptied voiders and glasses were removed and replaced by fresh supplies.

Other voiders of this period were of wainscot. This was the kind of small woodwork that developed into a souvenir craft in such centres as Tunbridge Wells. As early as 1727 Mrs. Pendarves wrote to her sister telling her that she was sending "Tunbridge Voiders". Such voiders (this spelling is consistent on the eighteenth-century trade cards) were advertised in the mid-eighteenth century by Francis Thompson, St. John's Lane, London.

Mahogany voiders had appeared on fashionable dessert tables by the 1740s. Chippendale in the 1754 edition of his *Director* illustrates four designs. But already the emphasis was changing and these are designs "for Tea-Trays or Voiders", although Ince & Mayhew in their *Universal System*, 1759–62, illustrate two patterns still captioned merely as "voiders".

These voiders varied in length from 24 to 30 inches and were about 18 inches wide. The encircling gallery, about 3 inches deep, was pierced—"cutt voiders" was the contemporary term. This carving still retains its edges as sharply crisp as new when worked in the hard, unstained San Domingo mahogany. In a fine example the corners were canted, the gallery pierced and carved, sometimes with such motifs as scrolling acanthus foliage. More frequently the galleries were pierced geometrically and the handles consisted of boldly out-curving scrolls with or without handholds: these were carved from the solid and not attached.

The trade card of Alexander Wetherstone, in Sir Ambrose Heal's collection, described him in about 1760 as "Carpenter, Joyner and Turner, Portugal St., Near Lincoln's Inn Back Gate", and announced that he made "Voiders, Tea Boards, Tea Trays, and Hand Boards", thus distinguishing between the four varieties of mahogany trays then fashionable. Sweetmeat voiders continued to be made until the 1790s.

The fashionable hostess of the early eighteenth century served tea from a silver tea-equipage composed of kettle and spirit lamp, tea-pot, pair of tea canisters, milk jug and sugar bowl arranged on a rectangular silver tray nearly 24 inches long and supported on four short feet. These trays were described in inventories of the period as "solid silver tea tables", and stood upon flat rimless boards of fine wood sunk with sockets to contain the tray feet. These were known as tea-boards. They were baize covered beneath and intended to protect drawing-room tables from the heat of the tea equipage, continuing to be used as late as the 1760s. The inventory of the Earl of Warrington's tea room taken in 1752 refers to "2 Mahogany stands to set the silver Tea and Coffee Tables on".

For the many who could not afford a silver tea-table, the board itself was adapted to take the tea-equipage. This, while it remained a single flat plank, although shaped with a raised rim and handles, still retained the name tea-board. It might be rectangular or scalloped. Joseph Patterson, turner, at the Crown in New Bond Street, London, announced on his trade card of about 1730 that he made "mahogany round tea boards". Frederick Hintz, Newport Street, London, advertised in the *Daily Post* during 1738 that he made mahogany tea-boards "curiously inlaid with fine figures of Brass and Mother-of-Pearl".

Many tea-boards were sunk with plainly turned rims. A typical example, measuring $18\frac{1}{4}$ inches in diameter and $\frac{13}{16}$-inch deep from rim to base, was found to weigh three

188

pounds. From about 1740 some were turned with plain convex rims carved with raised radiating flutes: in others the rims might be moulded or reeded. The tea-board with a scalloped rim was fashionable, too, shaped and sunk from a single piece of mahogany on a specially designed lathe. This was hand-finished, but seldom hand-worked throughout. The eight-scalloped tea-board was popular and in good work the inner curves of the scallops met in meticulously carved points. Among the Hoare collection of bills in the Victoria and Albert Museum is one from "John Pardoe, the Cabinet and Chair, next to Temple Barr in ye Strand" for an "8-scalloped mahogany tea-board". The trade card of William Russell, a mahogany turner and cabinet-maker of the 1770s, illustrates a fourteen-scallop tea-board.

The so-called pie-crust outline was widely borrowed from the silversmiths, the contrasting curves and points of the cyma outline proving as brilliantly successful in high quality mahogany as in silver. It was cut from the solid on the scalloping machine and hand-finished, and apparently was known to Georgian turners merely as a "scallop rim". Bailey's dictionary, 1730, defined "scollop" as "a sort of Indenting of any Thing". Late eighteenth-century pie-crust tea-boards were less deeply indented than earlier examples.

It is evident from contemporary trade card announcements that by the mid-eighteenth century the terms tray and board were clearly differentiated. A board had a lathe-fashioned rim; a tray had an applied rim shaped with the tools of the cabinet-maker. This differentiation appears to date from about 1740. The trade card of "Thomas Hollinshed, Turner, Ye Corner of Great Queen Street, Drury Lane, London", issued in the mid-1750s, announced that he made "Mahogany and Walnuttree Trays and Tea Boards". Thirty years later Richard Holmes advertised "all Sorts of Cutt Trays, Scollop and Round Tea Boards".

The Royal Account Books at Buckingham Palace show that in 1762 William Vile supplied "2 Neat Mahogany Tea Boards with rims all Round for the Queen's House in the Park at St. James's" and "an octagon tray, with a cutt work rim". In this instance the contrast in price is also known: the turned tea-board cost 24s. and the cabinet-made tray cost 48*s*. Tea-boards continued to be used throughout the Georgian period.

Small versions of tea-boards, known originally as hand-boards or waiting-boards, were used by servants for handing small objects such as letters or drinks. By the mid-eighteenth century they were known as waiters, a term acquired from the silversmiths. Thomas Chapman in 1770 advertised that he made "Mahogany Tea Boards, Waiters". An early Georgian hand-board was often just a square of wainscot with a hand-sunk centre and a convex rim, rounded, clipped or indented at the corners. In some instances it was merely a flat board with an applied moulded rim. More fashionably it was japanned and enriched with gilded ornament, like the larger voider. Lady Grisell Baillie in 1715 paid five shillings for "a Japan Lief to hand about Tee". In mahogany such boards were turned in the lathe, round or scalloped, until the end of the eighteenth century, reduced versions of the tea-board. The term hand-board has been noted as late as 1770.

Tray was defined by Bailey in 1730 as "a sort of Vessel or Trough hollowed out of a Piece of Wood, used by Butchers". Its widespread use in connection with the service of tea appears to date from the 1760s when wooden tea-trays became fashionable tea-time accessories. They were constructed with applied galleries measuring no more than 2 inches deep. Inevitably at this period of elliptical, neo-classical form the tea-tray was oval, in the silversmith's manner. Ince & Mayhew, for instance, illustrate one with a pierced vertical gallery and boldly scrolling handles at the narrow ends, perhaps the earliest example of an oval tray in the cabinet-makers' pattern books.

Eventually the oval tea-tray became a cabinet-maker's speciality. At first the rims were cut in lattice-work designs and mounted around plain boards selected for the fine figuring of the grain. With the demand for inlay and marquetry in colourful woods the boards of tea-trays from about 1770 became highly ornamental. Grounds of mahogany, satinwood, harewood or kingwood veneer were set with marquetry in contrasting light-coloured woods such as box and holly, and colourful imported or stained woods.

Designs were largely restricted to the well-known neo-classical patterns such as urn, shell and fan shapes. Such simple patterns could be sand-burnt into oval medallions of holly and surrounded by outer bands of contrasting woods. Marquetry men specialised in supplying such motifs.

Hepplewhite in his *Guide*, 1788, illustrates several fashionable trays, the finest without handles, and some with the gallery edge cut in undulating long and short scallops. Hepplewhite wrote in this connection: "For Tea Trays a great variety of patterns may be invented and almost any kind of ornament introduced." From this period painted and varnished tea-trays were fashionable too. These were less costly than the marquetry work, but both continued in wide demand until about 1810. A tea-tray of this period, like the tea-pots and other equipage it bore, might be larger than formerly, sometimes as much as 36 inches long and 21 inches wide. The gallery was plain and from about 1790 its top edge might be inlaid with stringing.

Metal handle grips began to be fitted from the early 1770s in silver and in gilded brass. They extended almost horizontally from the tray, the ends running beneath the base into which they were sunk level with the under-surface of the wood: later handles gripped the rim with fork-like attachments. Handle grips tended to rise vertically above the galleries from about 1790. By 1790 tea-trays might be more narrowly elliptical with D-handles extending outward, offering more space for the fingers, and given a slight twist, perhaps, to make the grip more secure.

Sheraton in his *Cabinet Dictionary*, 1803, detailed many trays and noted that mahogany dinner trays with galleries 3½ inches in depth "were now used for taking up dishes and plates to the dinner table". The tray rims remained about 2 inches deep. The oval tea-tray was succeeded by the rectangular form from about 1810 with elaborately cast handles of silver or gilded brass. Trays of this period might be inlaid with scrollwork and foliated ornament in brass or ebonised wood.

It is worthy of note that the pivoted tea-tray dates no earlier than 1816 when John Hawkins patented "improvements on tea-boards or tea trays, consisting in making them turn on a pivot, so that the cups may be turned to the proper party".

Trays in mahogany designed especially for use by butlers date from the the mid-eighteenth century onwards. Some early examples were handsome pieces, with ornamentally pierced galleries. On 14th June 1756 Daniel Mason, Cabinet Maker, Golden Ball, Newport Street, London, charged the Earl of Winterton twelve shillings for "a Larg Mahogy Butlers Trea with Brass Corners". Such trays were obviously rectangular and were made *en suite* with pail plate carriers and voiders. A trestle-style folding stand was introduced to receive the laden tray. In some instances the X-shaped legs and stretchers were pierced with lattice-work decoration to match that on the tray. By the 1770s the oval butler's tray had appeared, the gallery constructed from short coopered staves bound with brass hoops. In some the handle grips were cut into the centres of the sides.

Sheraton in his *Cabinet Dictionary* wrote of butlers' trays: "These trays are made of mahogany, half-inch Honduras will do for the sides, but the bottoms ought always to be made of Spanish or other hard wood, otherwise the glasses and slop will leave such a print on soft wood, as cannot be easily erased." He added that one end should be made nearly open "for the convenience of having easy access to the glasses". This was a very popular type of butler's tray and is usually found with a X stand. A point that may help in dating such a stand is the change from mainly rectangular legs and stretchers to mainly turned members. This occurred around 1810.

Chapter Twenty-four

WINE CISTERNS AND CELLARETS

W INE cisterns filled with iced water played an ostenta-
tious part in banqueting ceremonial from Tudor to
early Victorian days, and were dining-room necessities
throughout the Georgian period. Bottles of wine immersed
in the ice-cold water were kept cool in an ill-ventilated
atmosphere usually overheated by a blazing fire and dozens
of wax candle flames.

It is probable that early wine cisterns were of thick copper
or latten plate. A conversation manual, *The French Garden:
for English Ladies and Gentlemen to walke in*, 1605, records
cisterns of two types and distinguishes between them. The
mistress of the house orders her butler to "put cleane and
fresh water in the tubbes, that of copper, the other of wood,
the one to keepe the drinke fresh, and the other to refresh
the glasses and cuppes, to the ende that we may drink fresh
for it is very hot".[1] Pepys cast an envious glance at a wine
cistern and wrote in his *Diary*, 1667, "I see the price of a
copper cistern for the table, which is very pretty, and they
demand £6 or £7 for one". There is evidence, however,
that wood cisterns large enough to contain several bottles of
wine were already in use. These were staved oval receptacles, made by coopers from narrow Baltic oak clap-
boards, riven and hooped with iron or latten.

The splendour and luxury in house furnishings which
followed the restoration of the Stewart regime in 1660
called for capacious wine cisterns of silver. Such a gorgeous
production would be placed beneath the service table
which might hold a matching wine fountain. Silver wine
cisterns were costly objects: Luttrell in 1695 mentioned

[1] *Dictionary of English Furniture*: Ralph Edwards, 1954.

193

"a sylver cystern, worth above £700, is stole from Berkley House".

These silver cisterns were oval and might measure more than 30 inches in length and 18 inches in height. The shallow body was usually embossed with ovolos or convex flutes rising from the base, and a band of embossed ornament —usually gadrooning—encircled the neck and the wide everted rim edged with decorative moulding. The body was supported by four superb cast and chased claw-and-ball feet, and the splendid appearance was completed by highly ornate handles such as female forms, perhaps, or seated lions with substantial lifting loops swinging from their paws.

Apollo in 1708 discussed "bottles of claret in a silver cistern of ice". The early eighteenth-century silver wine cistern retained the oval bowl, slightly deeper than before, and strengthened with ornamental cut-card work around the lower part. It was supported on a spreading foot ring, its edge encircled with gadrooning, matching similar decoration on the bowl rim. Ovolo embossment around the body continued, however. Handles might be in the form of fixed scrolls or double scrolls, their upper edges supporting cast and chased crests modelled in the round.

The early Georgians copied silver cisterns in marble, porphyry and granite. Isaac Ware and William Kent, when designing furnishings for Sir Robert Walpole's parlour at Houghton, Suffolk, in about 1730, included a large granite cistern before one of the side tables. Water remained cold longer in stone cisterns than in silver so that ice was required less frequently. The early stone cistern stood upon a low pedestal foot of similar material: by 1730 it was set in strong oval rings of mahogany supported by four out-curving lion-paw legs linked by deep carved aprons.

Wine cisterns shaped in mahogany appeared in the 1730s, close adaptations of silver and marble forms. Thus the silversmith's design was translated into a cabinet-maker's medium *via* the stone mason. Such a cistern was cut in the solid from a balk of mahogany, with a projecting rim, and with a slab of marble set in the base. The exterior might be encircled with straight or spiral ovolos or enriched with deep rococo carving, the design standing in high relief. In some examples the bowl rested upon a low oval foot turned separately, acanthus leaf motifs encircling the bowl base and foot rim.

More frequently the cistern was set in a stand, with four strong cabriole legs carved with acanthus leaf ornament at the shoulder, and with paw or claw-and-ball feet. Other legs had flowering scrolls extending outward at the top, giving the effect of setting back the aprons. Most of these cisterns were ornamented with ovolo carving, the rim curving outward to the same extent as the sweep of the ovolo, with a stepped-up lip.

Thomas Chippendale on the title page of his *Director* includes "Cisterns for Water" in his list of designs, and also illustrates four examples captioned "Four Cisterns. The ornaments should be of Brass. The Cistern at Bottom [of the group] should be made of Wood or Marble, and cut out of the Solid. The others may be made in parts, joined with Brass work".

The mahogany wine cistern of the mid-eighteenth century, more capacious than formerly, was built from four sections of wood, two slightly curved sides and two deeply bowed ends. The lower edges were curved inward to receive an inserted base. The plain outer surface might be enriched with a carved encircling rib centrally placed to conceal a joint in the wood: the rim also was carved in a matching pattern. At each end was a heavy swing handle moulded in a pinchbeck type of alloy and double gilded. These handles were attached in such a way that the cistern, made water-tight with a closely fitting lead lining, could be lifted from its stand, then a separate unit.

Wine cisterns until the 1760s were necessarily expansive to contain a number of wide bottles then measuring 6 or more inches in diameter. These were short bodied and the cistern was therefore shallow, the iced water immersing them to the shoulders. In the 1760s the wine bottle became taller with a slightly tapering neck and a cylindrical body measuring about 5 inches in diameter. During the 1770s and 1780s the body was reduced to about 4 inches in diameter, taller than formerly, with a tapering neck, and from the early 1790s it seldom exceeded 3½ inches in diameter.

During this half century the fashionable wine cistern required frequent re-designing to bring it to a depth capable of even half immersing the taller bottles in iced water.

This brought into fashionable use the brass-bound oval mahogany cistern in the style the joiners had long been making in Baltic oak for use in coaching houses, tavernsl assembly halls and so on, such as are illustrated in several of Hogarth's paintings. These continued in production unti, Victorian days but might also be used for other purposes, particularly in the brew house.

It has been suggested that staved wine cisterns of mahogany were the work of coopers. This is unlikely for the cooper's technique and tools differ entirely from those of the joiner who made these cisterns. Alexander Wetherstone, carpenter, joiner and turner, whose trade card of about 1760 was mentioned in the previous chapter, recorded that he "sold Mahogany Cisterns with Brass hoops". The hoops, of course, were a safeguard in the event of dampness affecting the mahogany.

Made of weighty mahogany, the staved cistern usually had a plainly rounded rim although gadrooned or other carved beading might be applied. It was hooped with broad bands of latten top and bottom, the latten being made from ingot brass hammered into sheets by the battery process, giving it a strong, tough texture. Usually from the 1770s, and invariably from about 1790, rolled brass was used for this purpose, thinner and less tough in texture. The staved cistern might then have a central band of brass shaped and pierced into an ornamental pattern, between two narrow bands. In many instances the brass is golden yellow in colour, showing it to have been made by the Emerson process dating from the 1770s. The upper hoop was fitted each end with a massive lion-mask ring-handle, at first of gilded brass, later of Emerson brass coated with lacquer. The cistern was provided with a lining hammered from sheet lead and fitted inside with a hinged D-handle at each end.

Hooped cisterns of mahogany might be carried on mahogany stands fitted with castors. Cabriole legs were frequent, including the less pronounced "French leg", with

196

finely carved shoulder and some on hoof feet. These might be enriched with touches of gilding to harmonise with the brass bands above. Less costly legs might be square with bracket corners of fret-work in the mid-eighteenth century Chinese manner; later tapered legs were used.

Under the neo-classical influence the oval staved wine cistern might be enriched top and bottom with wide bands of mahogany inlaid with decoration in some lighter-hued wood. Each of the long sides might be interrupted by the insertion of an ornamental panel such as an urn or other classical motif carved in low relief against a ground of satinwood. Directly to the base were attached four tapering legs of square section terminating in castors. Beneath the mahogany banding of a damaged example noted was a narrower encircling hoop of steel.

By the 1780s the stand might be dispensed with, the base hoop then being lowered to floor level. In some instances the sides had an outward splay towards the rim and the two end staves were carried above the rim and curved into a pair of lifting handles. A central hoop of brass might also be fitted. More frequently a hooped cistern had vertical sides, the upper band, about 2 inches below the rim, being fitted with a pair of heavy brass lifting handles hinging to lion masks. These continued in use in late Georgian days, as shown in Henry Alken's after-the-hunt drawing "The Toast", 1828. Examples are sometimes noted with fixed linings of zinc. These must be dated after the late 1820s when rolled sheet zinc was first produced.

The wine cistern by the end of the eighteenth century was becoming a pretentious piece of carved furniture. Sheraton in his *Cabinet Dictionary*, 1803, termed his designs sarcophagus wine cisterns, illustrating two and describing them as "in faint degree, an imitation of the figure of the ancient stone coffins, on which account only can the term be justified". This floridly carved container was generally of mahogany with a fixed lining of lead: it stood upon four heavy paw feet or upon a thick, shaped mahogany plinth.

The introduction of taller wine bottles in the 1760s also resulted in the manufacture of square or rectangular wine cisterns fitted with lead linings and standing on four legs.

Weight was considerably reduced, enabling them to be moved easily on castors. Later such a cistern was divided into nine sections, the centre one containing ice, and a separate stand was used.

Wine cistern making was usually the province of specialist cabinet-makers, frequently working for one of the larger firms. A trade card in Sir Ambrose Heal's collection, issued by "Dalziel of the Chair, Corner of Wych Street, facing Drury Lane", announces that he made mahogany cisterns, and illustrates two fashionable examples of the period. One is circular, the other octagonal, each divided into eight bottle compartments radiating from a central ice compartment, and resting on four substantial paw or scroll feet. By the end of the 1770s such a cistern was fitted with a hinged lid and fastened with a lock. These are described in Hepplewhite's *Guide*, 1788: "Cellarets also called *gardes du vin*, are generally made of mahogany, hooped with brass lacquered: the inner part is divided with partitions, and lined with lead, for bottles. They may be of any shape and are in general use where sideboards are without drawers." Hepplewhite illustrates two flat-lidded examples, oval and octagonal, on stands with four plainly square tapered legs which may have spade feet. The apron of the stand may be encircled with a band of plainly carved fluting. The container is shown constructed from picturesquely grained mahogany hooped with wide bands of brass, the upper hoop being pierced by a keyhole, immediately above a mask ring handle matching two others at the sides. The veneer on the lid is set in segments. The interior contains the customary eight bottle compartments with a central iced water compartment fitted with a brass draw-off tap.

Early in the 1790s three brass hoops were preferred. One, narrow or broad, encircled the lid-rim, and two broad ones were used high and low on the body. The upper half of the stand was now enclosed and formed a receptacle for glasses and decanters. By the beginning of the nineteenth century the stand might be entirely enclosed, with a door in front giving access to storage space supported on four bracket feet and castors. *The Footman's Directory*, 1825, advised butlers always to "keep a supply of proper corks in the cellaret".

Sheraton's *Cabinet Dictionary* distinguishes between spirit cellarets "made to hold square bottles, and wine cellarets which are not made strictly to the dimensions of the bottles but large enough to hold six, eight or ten round wine bottles and have an ornamental appearance". Each compartment might contain a different wine, enabling the host to offer a selection. Two years later Sheraton wrote that cellarets "are not so generally used as they were, and amongst the higher classes are wholly laid aside . . ." in favour of silver wine coolers for the table. Yet J. Beresford in *Miseries of Human Life*, 1806, recounted

" . . . With venturous hands,
At the cellaret stands,
Where she picks out so handy
Rum, Hollands and Brandy."

The term *garde du vin* continued in use. A writer in *Blackwood's Magazine*, 1827, in discussing the servant problem, remarked "your purse, your gardevin, and your tea caddy are continually exposed to depredation". The term might also be spelled gardyveen.

A rare type of cellaret was in the outline of a gothic arch supported on four short tapered legs fitted with socket castors. A flat, cusp-shaped door at the front hinged downward, giving access to six horizontal sections for bottles. Two examples noted were intended for the 3½ inch Regency bottle.

The mahogany wine-waiter was a nineteenth-century innovation. This was a deep, open, oblong tray divided into sections for individual bottles, with a central hand-grip, and supported on four plain legs running on castors.

Chapter Twenty-five

NEEDLEWOMEN until the mid-Georgian period carried their numerous sewing and embroidery requisites in baskets specially designed for the purpose and usually covered with decorative textile. The work in hand, such as hangings and heavy clothing, was kept in a larger basket. Both baskets were fitted with hasp and loop for padlocking against inquisitive fingers. These inelegant-looking baskets in the late 1760s began to be superseded by cabinet-made pouch tables of mahogany.

The earliest example illustrated in *The Dictionary of English Furniture* is at Osterley Park and attributed to about 1770. This is in grey painted beech carved with neo-classic motifs enriched with gilding. The table top, painted with a representation of the firmament, measures about 18 inches by 13 inches and hinges open from the frieze, giving immediate access to an 18-inch deep pleated green silk pouch for containing needlework. This can be locked and there is, of course, no drawer. Needlework accessories still remained in a basket which stood on a shelf fitted below the pouch between the four slender square legs with cabriole curves and scroll feet.

In some instances the basket was supported on a separate stand such as was described in 1786 by Sophie von la Roche: "I will just mention the neat stands for work-baskets which have just arrived at Lady Fieldings, consisting of three smooth round legs made of mahogany, or any other wood attractively painted, placed next to one another and fastened. [This was known as a cat, its six legs or spokes radiating from a central sphere so that the stand always rested upon three legs.] The pretty embroidered work-baskets placed on them in a corner of the room form a charming decoration; and they are very convenient to carry to and fro for working purposes and take up very little space."

Mahogany pouch tables were made, displaying features associated with Chippendale, their height approximating 30 inches, a measurement convenient for a lady seated. Strangely, most cabinet-makers' design books of the eighteenth century ignore pouch tables. An example, formerly in the collection of Earl Howe, has a top in serpentine outline edged with gadrooning hinged to a frieze of mock lattice work. Pouch tables were also made in walnut and satinwood with square tapering legs and without the basket shelf. The tops of walnut tables were enriched with floral marquetry: satinwood might be painted with colourful figure subjects. In some there is a sliding screen at the back to protect the face of the needlewoman from the fire. Oval pouch tables were also fashionable. The Duke of Devonshire possesses two, the pleated pouches fringed around the lower edge and one with a work-box shelf.

Sheraton in his *Drawing Book*, 1791–3, continued the design that provided direct access to the pouch. By now the pouch was lined with pliable leather and the pleated silk covering fashionably "hidden by festoons of fringed drapery", its frame "commonly made of satinwood with brass moulding round the edge of the rim". He illustrates two examples, the lids of both enriched with all-over painted designs. One has a kidney-shaped top, the square central portion hinged to form a reading desk: when let down this locks into the frame and prevents unauthorised entrance to the pouch. The lobes at the ends have narrow drawers let into the frieze. From the trestle legs lyre-shaped uprights rise to support the frame, tenoned to transverse pieces screwed to its underside. A work-box shelf encircled by a low open-work gallery connects the uprights at the trestle junctions.

The second example is oval. The top is hinged to a frieze 2 inches deep, which is made separately and supported by tenoned uprights rising from a round frame with cross-stretchers of wainscot. The junction of these rests on a pillar rising from four out-spreading convex legs. The silk pouch is ornamented with drapery.

Table, pouch and work-box were combined into a single piece of furniture during the 1790s. The earliest record so far noted of such a work-table is to be seen in the 1795 cost book of the Gillow firm, Lancaster. This illustrates a tripod-pillar type with a fixed top and hinged side flaps. In the frieze is a shallow drawer for needlework equipment, the pouch being suspended below from a pull-out slide.

This type is more commonly found in mahogany and satinwood, with a fixed table top covering a drawer in the frieze, on four outward raking legs, square and tapered. A shell or patera might be inlaid in the centre of the top and others in the blocks above the legs. By the end of the century the leg design might be six-sided and tapering, square at the top above a turned neck, and ending in a turned foot. In others trestle feet supported a pair of pierced or solid lyre-shaped end-pieces or four turned uprights.

By 1803, when Sheraton published his *Cabinet Dictionary*, the work-table had become even more comprehensive. The frieze had been deepened and the table top again hinged to cover a work-box fitted with compartments and loose receptacles for needlework accessories. Below was a drawer similarly laid out, and the pull-out pouch was suspended below. Sheraton referred to such furniture as a pouch table which he defined as one with "a bag, used by ladies to work at, in which they deposit their fancy needlework, The work-bags are suspended on a frame which draws forward, in which frame is a lock which shuts its bolt into the under edge of the rail above. They are also used as chess tables occasionally . . . the frets on the edges of the tables are of brass, and the ground ought to be of black rosewood when they are required to be elegant, otherwise they may be very neatly made of mahogany".

Sheraton refers to "M'Lean, of Mary le bone Street" as a skilful maker of pouch tables. This was the firm of John Mclean & Son whose trade card describes them as "Upholder and Cabinet-maker, on the Upper Terrace, Tottenham Court Road and Marylebone Street", and specialists in "Elegant Parisian Furniture".

The fashionable woods of the early nineteenth century included rosewood, often crossbanded and inlaid with satin-wood, and ebonised stringing. Satinwood might be used, inlaid with mahogany or ebonised stringing, or maple wood banded with mahogany and inlaid with checker pattern lines. Rosewood and satinwood might be inlaid with mother-of-pearl; mahogany with brass or mother-of-pearl.

In some instances a pouch work-table possessed two drawers below the box, all divided into compartments, some with lids, others containing small circular or square boxes. These were lined with silk, or, after about 1820, with decorative paper. The drawers were fitted with brass lever locks and knobs, at first in brass, later in turned wood or bone. Examples are known fitted with musical boxes.

Pouch work-tables have been noted in which the drawer contains a book-rest flanked by recesses for sewing equipment. In these the pouch instead of drawing forward slides to the left. The hinged top, either rectangular or oval, might cover a lifting tray of accessories fitting into the silk-lined recess. In some instances the end friezes of a rectangular top contained two small drawers. Size gradually increased. A width of 18 inches was normal until the 1790s when it gradually increased until 24 inches became usual by 1820. A reversion to the smaller size had occurred by the 1850s.

Combination game and work tables were fashionable during the first quarter of the nineteenth century, many following the design illustrated by Sheraton on plate 65 of his *Cabinet Dictionary*. In the standard type the central portion of the top was made to slide off, revealing a tric-trac and backgammon board in the recess. The reverse of the slide-off top was inlaid in a checker pattern for chess and draughts. In some oval tables the two semi-circular ends were galleried and hinged, forming the lids of containers for game pieces and playing cards.

During the Regency years 1810–20 there was a vogue for a globe-shaped work-table. This was supported on three deeply convex legs of square section topped by ram's head masks of ormolu and with gilded feet mounted on a heavy triangular plinth with moulded concave edges. The upper half of the hollow mahogany or rosewood globe, measuring

26 inches in diameter, swung backward and downward exposing a ring of compartments around the inner perimeter, the centre being open and giving access to the lower half of the globe which acted as a pouch. Instead of a globe, a low tripod of this type might support hemispherical or four-cornered open cage-work to receive a rectangular or kidney-shaped box, its frieze ornamented with stringing, and the lid interior fitted with an oval or rectangular mirror.

The Regency furniture-makers also followed the French fashion of setting the tops of pouch work-tables with marble or scagliola. An example illustrated in *Ackermann's Repository*, 1809, is described as having a marble top, whilst the pouch, instead of being in the usual silk or lutestring, consisted of "a network of silk forming a bag for ladies' work". Silk network was the fashion until about 1820 when pleated silk became usual.

Loudon's *Encyclopaedia* records that the fashionable pouch table of the early 1830s had trestle legs supporting sturdy reeded balusters. The rectangular top was not hinged but the drawer was more capacious than formerly. The heavy pedestal type with box, drawer and pouch continued to be made, usually with a heavy triangular plinth in which castors might be concealed. In some instances the top was made to swivel.

These forms were superseded during the 1840s by designs in which the pouch was concealed within a hexagonal or octagonal cone of well-marked wood—most popularly walnut or maple wood, although mahogany, rosewood and satinwood were also used, and in lesser numbers, yew, zebra-wood and kingwood. The hinged lid contained a mirror and opened to give access to a lift-out tray of accessories, with a well below for needlework.

Work-tables originally intended to accompany pouch tables were made by cabinet-makers from the early 1780s until 1810. The design consisted of a rectangular tray top with deep galleries, the front hinged and secured vertically by means of two brass thumb springs. Below were one or two oval or canoe-shaped trays extending between a pair of vase-shaped supports which might be pierced or solid. They were illustrated by Sheraton as "French work tables" and measured about 24 inches wide. Early examples were of "satinwood veneered over inch stuff" with brass moulding covering the edges of the rims. Work-tables of the early nineteenth century were in mahogany or rosewood.

INDEX

(Plates are indicated by italic figures.)

INDEX